PIPE FITTINGS

NIPPLES

PIPE LENGTHS UP TO 22 FT.

STRAIGHT COUPLING

REDUCING COUPLING

COUPLING

NUT

CAP

STRAIGHT TEE

REDUCING TEE

STREET TEE

STRAIGHT CROSS

REDUCING CROSS

90° ELBOW

90° ELBOW

90° ELBOW

45° ELBOW

REDUCING ELBOW

90° STREET ELBOW

45° STREET ELBOW

45° Y-BEND

UNION (3 PARTS)

PLUG

BUSHING

CAP

RETURN BEND

REDUCING TEE

REDUCER

90°

45°
UNION ELBOWS

STREET

UNION TEES

PLUG

45° ELBOW

TEE

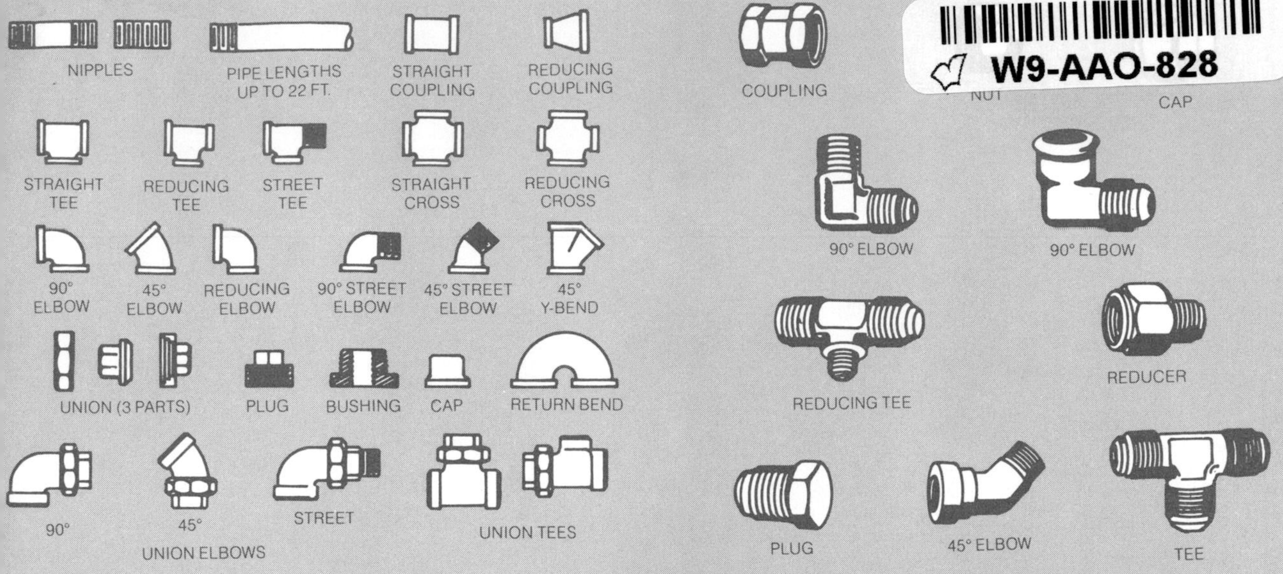

MEASURES OF CAPACITY

1 cup	=	8 fl oz
2 cups	=	1 pint
2 pints	=	1 quart
4 quarts	=	1 gallon
2 gallons	=	1 peck
4 pecks	=	1 bushel

STANDARD STEEL PIPE ((All Dimensions in inches)

Nominal Size	Outside Diameter	Inside Diameter	Nominal Size	Outside Diameter	Inside Diameter
⅛	0.405	0.269	1	1.315	1.049
¼	0.540	0.364	1¼	1.660	1.380
⅜	0.675	0.493	1½	1.900	1.610
½	0.840	0.622	2	2.375	2.067
¾	1.050	0.824	2½	2.875	2.469

WOOD SCREWS

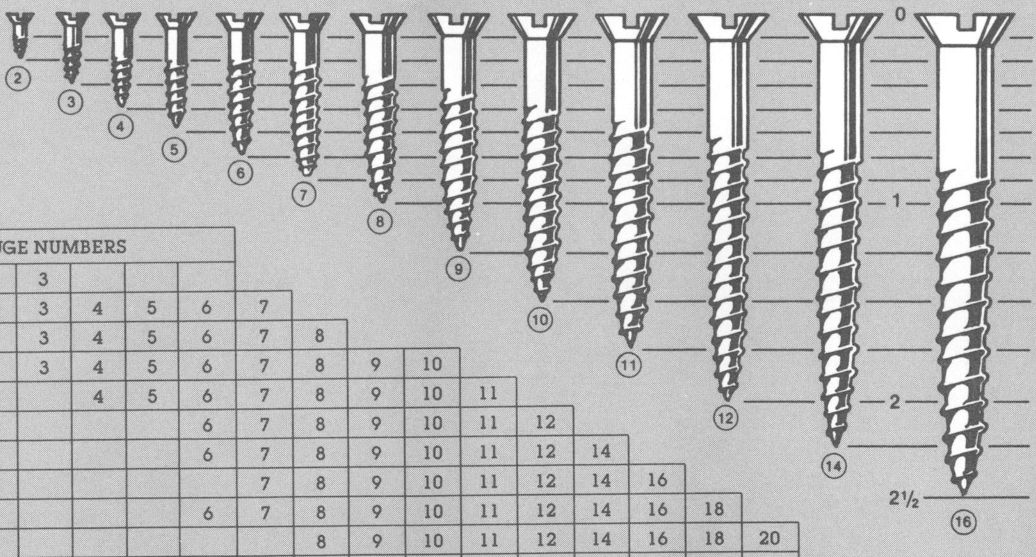

LENGTH	GAUGE NUMBERS																	
	0	1	2	3														
¼ INCH	0	1	2	3														
⅜ INCH			2	3	4	5	6	7										
½ INCH			2	3	4	5	6	7	8									
⅝ INCH				3	4	5	6	7	8	9	10							
¾ INCH					4	5	6	7	8	9	10	11						
⅞ INCH							6	7	8	9	10	11	12					
1 INCH							6	7	8	9	10	11	12	14				
1¼ INCH								7	8	9	10	11	12	14	16			
1½ INCH							6	7	8	9	10	11	12	14	16	18		
1¾ INCH									8	9	10	11	12	14	16	18	20	
2 INCH									8	9	10	11	12	14	16	18	20	
2¼ INCH										9	10	11	12	14	16	18	20	
2½ INCH													12	14	16	18	20	
2¾ INCH														14	16	18	20	
3 INCH															16	18	20	
3½ INCH																18	20	24
4 INCH																18	20	24

WHEN YOU BUY SCREWS, SPECIFY (1) LENGTH, (2) GAUGE NUMBER, (3) TYPE OF HEAD—FLAT, ROUND, OR OVAL, (4) MATERIAL—STEEL, BRASS, BRONZE, ETC., (5) FINISH—BRIGHT, STEEL BLUED, CADMIUM, NICKEL, OR CHROMIUM PLATED.

Popular Mechanics

do-it-yourself encyclopedia

The complete, illustrated home reference guide from the world's most authoritative source for today's how-to-do-it information.

Volume 2

AQUARIUMS
to
BATTERIES AND
STARTING SYSTEMS: AUTO

HEARST DIRECT BOOKS

NEW YORK

Acknowledgements

The Popular Mechanics Encyclopedia is published with the consent and cooperation of POPULAR MECHANICS Magazine.

For POPULAR MECHANICS Magazine:

Editor-in-Chief: *Joe Oldham*

Managing Editor: *Bill Hartford*

Special Features Editor: *Sheldon M. Gallager*

Automotive Editor: *Wade A. Hoyt, SAE*

Home and Shop Editor: *Steve Willson*

Electronics Editor: *Stephen A. Booth*

Boating, Outdoors and Travel Editor: *Timothy H. Cole*

Science Editor: *Dennis Eskow*

Popular Mechanics Encyclopedia

Project Director: *Boyd Griffin*

Manufacturing: *Ron Schoenfeld*

Assistant Editors: *Cynthia W. Lockhart Peter McCann, Rosanna Petruccio*

Production Coordinator: *Peter McCann*

The staff of Popular Mechanics Encyclopedia is grateful to the following individuals and organizations:

Editor: *C. Edward Cavert*

Editor Emeritus: *Clifford B. Hicks*

Production: *Layla Productions*

Production Director: *Lori Stein*

Book Design: *The Bentwood Studio*

Art Director: *Jos. Trautwein*

Design Consultant: *Suzanne Bennett & Associates*

Illustrations: *AP Graphics, Evelyne Johnson Associates, Popular Mechanics Magazine, Vantage Art.*

Contributing Writers: Manly Banister, *Bandsaw tips from the experts*, page 170; Rosario Capotosto, *Redwood barbecue cart*, page 175; *Wrap a table around your barbecue*, page 179; Rick Eickhoff, *Barbecue bar for your family room*, page 181; Paul Fiebach, *Rip fence for your bandsaw*, page 174; John Gaynor and Harry Wicks, *Finishing touches for basement remodeling*, page 194; Phil and Loretta Hermann, *Tiffany-style terrarium*, page 136; Wayne C. Leckey, *Party center bar you can build*, page 184; Leonard Sabal, *Aquarium coffee table*, page 132; Jeff Sandler, *Guide to small batteries*, page 235; Mort Schultz *Maintenance-free battery care*, page 249; Don Shiner, *Early American shaving console*, page 229; Tim Snider, *Bathroom projects*, page 202; *Technical tips*, page 204; *Fixtures and faucets*, page 206; *Bathroom finishing techniques*, page 208; George S. Watson, *Drop-on table for your bandsaw*, page 173; Harry Wicks, *Bandsaw basics*, page 167; Steve Willson and Steve Fay, *Remodeling a basement*, page 190.

Picture Credits: Popular Mechanics Encyclopedia is grateful to the following for permission to reprint their photographs: American Olean Tile Company—Barry Halkin Photography, page 203; American Olean Tile Company, pages 208 and 209; Karen Bussolini, pages 211 and 212; Delta Faucets, page 206 (right); Kohler Company, pages 206 (left), 207 (top) and 218.

ISBN 0-87851-155-5

Library of Congress 85-81760

10 9 8 7 6 5 4 3 2 1

PRINTED IN THE UNITED STATES OF AMERICA

Although every effort has been made to ensure the accuracy and completeness of the information in this book, Hearst Direct Books makes no guarantees, stated or implied, nor will they be liable in the event of misinterpretation or human error made by the reader, or for any typographical errors that may appear. WORK SAFELY WITH HAND TOOLS. WEAR SAFETY GOGGLES. READ MANUFACTURER'S INSTRUCTIONS AND WARNINGS FOR ALL PRODUCTS.

Contents

Aquarium coffee table

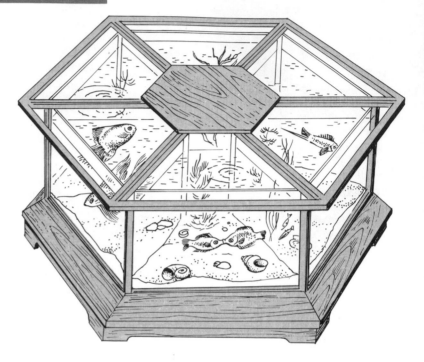

FASCINATING AQUARIUM TABLE is full of optical surprises if every other section is stocked—looking from an empty tank through a full tank lets you see the fish in the tank directly opposite you. Although all six tanks hold water, this alternating arrangement provides three compartments ideal for terrariums or displays. The table will hold 25 fish, and allows separation of different species. Pumps, etc., are in the center.

■ IF YOU'VE ALWAYS wanted a conversation piece for your living room or study, this coffee table or wall-mounted aquarium is the answer. It is, indeed, unique and you can be sure that you'll have your friends talking about it the first time you invite them in for an evening. Although it appears difficult to build, it isn't.

As you see on these pages, the table is divided into six separate compartments, each of which is sealed and completely independent of the others. The dry center well is also sealed and is an ideal location for the air pump, regulating valves and light fixture.

While the six sections can be used as separate aquariums, you can initially use three compartments to stock a generous number of tropical fish and set up the others as miniature gardens, terrariums or even model and trophy display cases.

The table is far less difficult to construct than it might appear. This is due in part to three factors: the absence of a reinforcing frame, use of a sealant that's also a bonding compound, and a totally symmetrical design.

Conventional aquariums are constructed of a slate bottom and glass sides, carefully fitted in a stainless-steel frame, and then sealed at all seams.

A relatively new type of sealant, however, makes it possible to bond glass directly to glass—without the steel frame—to produce strong, clean and leak-proof joints. The nontoxic sealant is basically a silicone rubber compound available in black, white and clear.

The symmetrical design of the table is what makes the unit relatively easy to construct. For

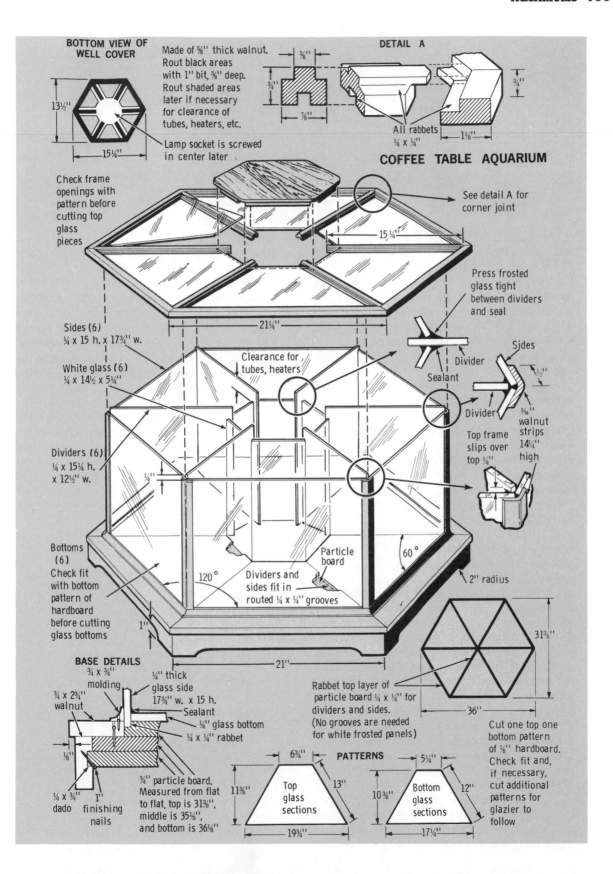

BOTTOM VIEW OF WELL COVER

13½"

15¼"

Made of ⅝" thick walnut. Rout black areas with 1" bit, ⅜" deep. Rout shaded areas later if necessary for clearance of tubes, heaters, etc.

Lamp socket is screwed in center later

DETAIL A

⅜"

¾"

¾"

⅞"

All rabbets ¼ x ¼"

1⅛"

COFFEE TABLE AQUARIUM

Check frame openings with pattern before cutting top glass pieces

See detail A for corner joint

15 ¼"

21¼"

Press frosted glass tight between dividers and seal

Sides (6) ¼ x 15 h. x 17¾" w.

White glass (6) ¼ x 14½ x 5¼"

Clearance for tubes, heaters

Divider

Sealant

Sides

Divider

½"

³⁄₁₆"

walnut strips 14¼" high

Top frame slips over top ¼"

Dividers (6) ¼ x 15¼ h. x 12½" w.

¼"

Bottoms (6) Check fit with bottom pattern of hardboard before cutting glass bottoms

1"

120°

Dividers and sides fit in routed ¼ x ¼" grooves

Particle board

60°

2" radius

21"

31³⁄₈"

36"

BASE DETAILS

¾ x ¾" molding

¾ x 2¾" walnut

⅛"

¼ x ¾" dado

1" finishing nails

¼" thick glass side 17¾" w. x 15 h.

Sealant

¼" glass bottom

¼ x ¼" rabbet

¾" particle board. Measured from flat to flat, top is 31³⁄₈", middle is 35⅛", and bottom is 36⅛"

Rabbet top layer of particle board ¼ x ¼" for dividers and sides. (No grooves are needed for white frosted panels)

Cut one top one bottom pattern of ⅛" hardboard. Check fit and, if necessary, cut additional patterns for glazier to follow

PATTERNS

6¾"

13"

11⅜"

Top glass sections

19¾"

5¼"

12"

10⅜"

Bottom glass sections

17¼"

DETAILS OF WELL CONSTRUCTION

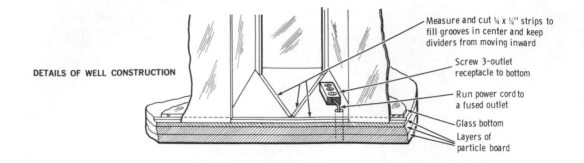

Measure and cut ¼ x ¼" strips to fill grooves in center and keep dividers from moving inward

Screw 3-outlet receptacle to bottom

Run power cord to a fused outlet

Glass bottom

Layers of particle board

this reason, the six sides, dividers and inner sides of white frosted glass can be cut to their respective sizes at the same time. In theory, all bottom panels should be identical, as should the top pieces, but because woodworking and glass-cutting tolerances can vary quite easily, cutting these pieces to fit is recommended. Other pieces can be off a bit since the design allows you to compensate for marginal errors.

Actual construction of the table will be tackled in three stages. First, assemble the lower half of the base; that is, the bottom two layers of particle board and the lower ring of ¾ x 2¾-in. strips of walnut. Then assemble the tank on the top layer of particle board and attach this to the lower part of the base. Finally, after testing the tank, add the tabletop frame, glass and well cover.

Glue and nail together the pieces for the lower part of the base, then cut the top layer of particle board to size (remember that 60° and 120° angles are used throughout). Rout the ¼ x ¼-in. grooves to the pattern shown (use a circular saw and jig if no router is available).

Fit the dividers and outside glass panels in the grooves and tape them together temporarily. Press a panel of white frosted glass between two dividers, clean the glass around this joint and seal the seams between the white panel and the dividers, *on the inside of the dry well only.* Prop the frosted panels so they will remain tight against the dividers and allow the sealant to dry overnight.

Measure and cut ¼ x ¼-in. wood strips to fill the grooves running inside the well from divider to divider. Then remove the glass sides and place the hardboard pattern for the glass bottom in each section. It should fit each opening within a $1/16$-in. margin. If the error is greater than $1/16$ in., cut additional patterns for the glazier to follow.

When all bottom glass panels fit properly, remove them one at a time and make certain that

glass and board are free of wood chips, drops of sealant, and such. Anything sandwiched between the two can cause the glass to crack later.

Now seal the bottom panels in place, beginning at an outer corner and running a continuous bead of sealant along the divider, frosted panel and the opposite divider. Then run another bead from the inner corners up along the seam of the frosted panel and the divider. Again, it's important to thoroughly clean all areas to be sealed.

Reposition the six outside panels on the grooved layer of particle board and check the corner joints between the sides and dividers before taping the sides securely in place. Then seal *all inside seams* between dividers, sides and bottoms. The outer seams and corners are sealed *after* the tank is set on the lower part of the base.

Let all sealed joints dry overnight before care-

TUBING AND POWER DETAILS

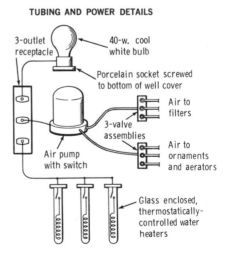

3-outlet receptacle

40-w. cool white bulb

Porcelain socket screwed to bottom of well cover

Air to filters

3-valve assemblies

Air pump with switch

Air to ornaments and aerators

Glass enclosed, thermostatically-controlled water heaters

fully positioning the tank on the base. Now cut and miter the top footing of ¾ x 2¾-in. walnut so that it fits snugly against the tank and overlaps the lower part of the base the same all around.

Glue and nail one section of the footing in place, then slide the tank away and apply sealant to the bottom outside joint. Slide the tank back up against the nailed section. Now apply sealant to the adjoining bottom seam, position the respective section of footing and nail this in place. Continue in this manner until all six sides are surrounded by the footing and then add the decorative curved molding to the footing.

Now remove the tape from the sides (one section at a time), fill the outside corner with sealant, add a little extra and press on the strip of matching walnut molding. Then firmly tape the strip tightly against the corner.

Remove the tape from the next corner joint, seal the outside seams, press on the walnut strip and retape. When all strips have been applied, wrap two or three turns of tape around the entire tank and let it dry undisturbed at least 24 hours.

You'll no doubt be in a hurry to fill the tank with water, but wait the full 24 hours and then move the tank to a flat spot, such as a patio or garage, where a drain and hose are available. Slowly fill each section of the tank with 4 to 6 inches of water, adding only an inch or so to each

section before going on to the next section. This procedure is important as it distributes the pressure evenly among the tank sections.

Turn off the water and examine the tanks for leaks. Mark any that are found with a grease pencil, drain the tank, cut away the sealant around the leak and reseal. Allow this tank to dry thoroughly before refilling. If you were careful with the initial sealing, however, you won't find any leaks. Just remember that the trick is to press a *continuous, unbroken bead* of sealant from corner to corner.

After this initial test, continue to add more water until the tanks are filled to within an inch of the top. Let the tanks remain under test and prepare the top frame and well cover. Fit these on the table, check the top glass pattern in each opening, and have the top pieces cut by a glazier. You can attach the frame to the dividers with sealant, but the top panels simply slip in and out of the frame for easy cleaning and access. Just be sure to dowel the spokes of the top frame to the outer members. An alternative to increase the strength of the frame is to screw metal plates underneath the frame joints.

The pump used in the table is a quiet vibrator model that will easily take care of all six tanks, including ornaments. Heaters, filters and ornaments are available at local aquarium shops.

Tiffany-style terrarium

■ MAKE THIS jewel-like "birdhouse" terrarium and fill it with your favorite ferns, mosses, African violets or other suitable house plants.

To begin, cut full-size paper patterns of the front and back sections. Secure them to glass using double-faced tape. Next, score the glass along the patterns' edges. The square sections can be marked on the glass with a grease pencil and scored with the aid of a straightedge.

For best results, hold the cutter as shown on the opposite page. The cutter's tip should be dipped in fine lubricating oil prior to making each cut. Draw the cutter toward you in one smooth and even stroke. Retrace only spots that the cutter skips. Avoid excessive pressure; it will leave small chips on the scored line and may cause erratic breaks. Curved sections of glass may be parted by tapping with the knob end of the cutter *under* the score. Pliers are also useful in forming the breaks (wear safety goggles).

Next, cut lengths of ⅜-in. copper foil tape long enough to encircle each cut piece, plus ¼ in. for overlap. Peel only a few inches of paper backing at a time. Center and apply the foil tape to the perimeters of the glass sections as shown. Rub tape on edges and sides with a burnishing stick to remove air bubbles.

To tin the foil, brush a thin coat of tinner's flux on the copper. (Try not to get flux on the glass because it may stain.) Then touch a small amount of 50/50 solid-core solder to a hot iron and quickly draw the molten solder along the foil.

Assemble the terrarium by arranging the front pieces on a flat surface and tacking them together. Center the front and back walls on the floor section and tack in place. Set each sidepiece on the same foundation and tack at the corners. Then tack roof sections in position.

Making beaded joints

To obtain beaded joints, touch the solder wire to the hot iron and move them along the seams without touching the foil. After soldering, wash the terrarium thoroughly with detergent to remove any acid.

For a bronzed, antique finish on the beading, brush a solution of copper sulfate and water onto the soldered edges. *Caution:* Copper sulfate is toxic, so wear rubber gloves. Give the terrarium a final scrubbing. Before planting, run a bead of silicone sealer around the lower seams.

After you've mastered Tiffany's technique, you may want to experiment with colored glass or mirror for other creations.

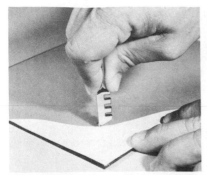

FULL-SIZE stencil cutouts give visual guide for scoring nonsquare sections.

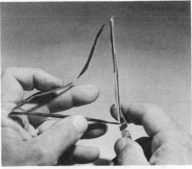

CUT COPPER foil strips long enough to wrap glass edges, adding ¼ in. overlap.

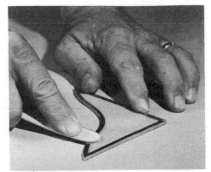

RUB ALL SURFACES of the foil with burnishing stick to remove air pockets.

APPLY THIN COAT of flux with acid brush. Then draw solder along foil.

LIGHTLY TACK corners until all pieces are in place.

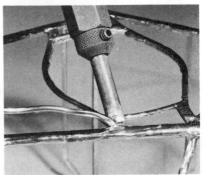

HOLD IRON'S TIP ⅛ in. above horizontal joint to form rounded edge bead.

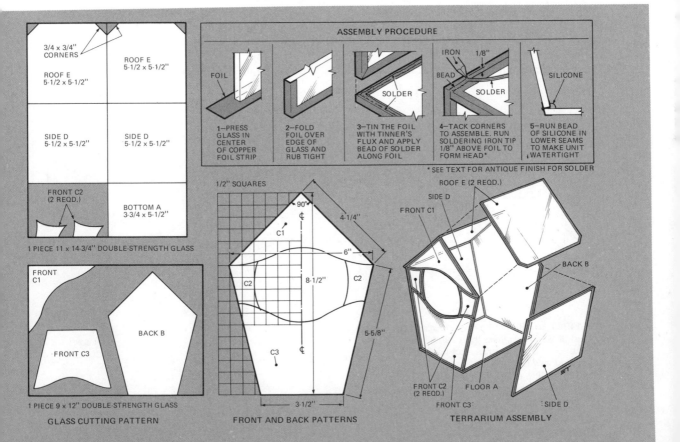

3/4 x 3/4'' CORNERS

ROOF E 5-1/2 x 5-1/2''

ROOF E 5-1/2 x 5-1/2''

SIDE D 5-1/2 x 5-1/2''

SIDE D 5-1/2 x 5-1/2''

FRONT C2 (2 REQD.)

BOTTOM A 3-3/4 x 5-1/2''

1 PIECE 11 x 14-3/4'' DOUBLE-STRENGTH GLASS

FRONT C1

BACK B

FRONT C3

1 PIECE 9 x 12'' DOUBLE-STRENGTH GLASS

GLASS CUTTING PATTERN

ASSEMBLY PROCEDURE

FOIL

1—PRESS GLASS IN CENTER OF COPPER FOIL STRIP

2—FOLD FOIL OVER EDGE OF GLASS AND RUB TIGHT

SOLDER

3—TIN THE FOIL WITH TINNER'S FLUX AND APPLY BEAD OF SOLDER ALONG FOIL

IRON 1/8''
BEAD
SOLDER

4—TACK CORNERS TO ASSEMBLE. RUN SOLDERING IRON TIP 1/8'' ABOVE FOIL TO FORM HEAD*

SILICONE

5—RUN BEAD OF SILICONE IN LOWER SEAMS TO MAKE UNIT WATERTIGHT

* SEE TEXT FOR ANTIQUE FINISH FOR SOLDER

1/2'' SQUARES

90°
C1
4-1/4''
6''
C2
8-1/2''
C2
5-5/8''
C3
3-1/2''

FRONT AND BACK PATTERNS

ROOF E (2 REQD.)
SIDE D
FRONT C1
BACK B
FRONT C2 (2 REQD.)
FLOOR A
FRONT C3
SIDE D

TERRARIUM ASSEMBLY

Attic dormer you can add to your home

■ WHEN A FAMILY starts outgrowing its house, moving to a larger one is not always the smart thing to do, especially if you have attic space that could be converted into the extra room you need.

Dormers play an important part in converting

attic space into a bedroom or two. They provide not only added headroom that's often required but light and air as well. Dormers can also do a lot to perk up an uninteresting roof line.

Whether you can take on the job of framing a dormer yourself depends a lot on how handy you

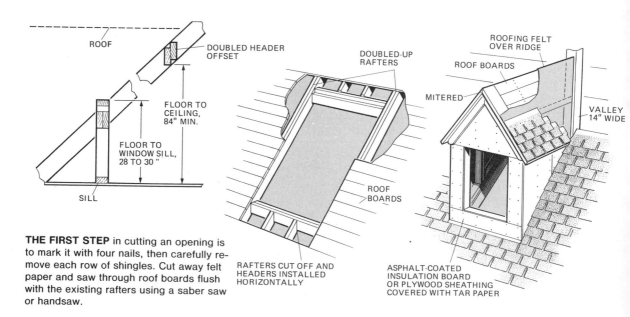

ROOF

DOUBLED HEADER OFFSET

FLOOR TO CEILING, 84" MIN.

FLOOR TO WINDOW SILL, 28 TO 30 "

SILL

DOUBLED-UP RAFTERS

ROOF BOARDS

ROOFING FELT OVER RIDGE

ROOF BOARDS

MITERED

VALLEY 14" WIDE

THE FIRST STEP in cutting an opening is to mark it with four nails, then carefully remove each row of shingles. Cut away felt paper and saw through roof boards flush with the existing rafters using a saber saw or handsaw.

RAFTERS CUT OFF AND HEADERS INSTALLED HORIZONTALLY

ASPHALT-COATED INSULATION BOARD OR PLYWOOD SHEATHING COVERED WITH TAR PAPER

IF FRAMING a dormer is too much for you to tackle even with the help of a friend, yet your attic remodeling plans require a dormer or two for adequate light and air, you can have this part of the overall job done while you take on the work inside. In seeking outside help, get bids from at least three contractors and compare prices. Ask each one for names of recent customers so you can get recommendations on their work. Insist on a comprehensive written contract with a complete description of the job, materials, timetable (especially important in this case) and payments.

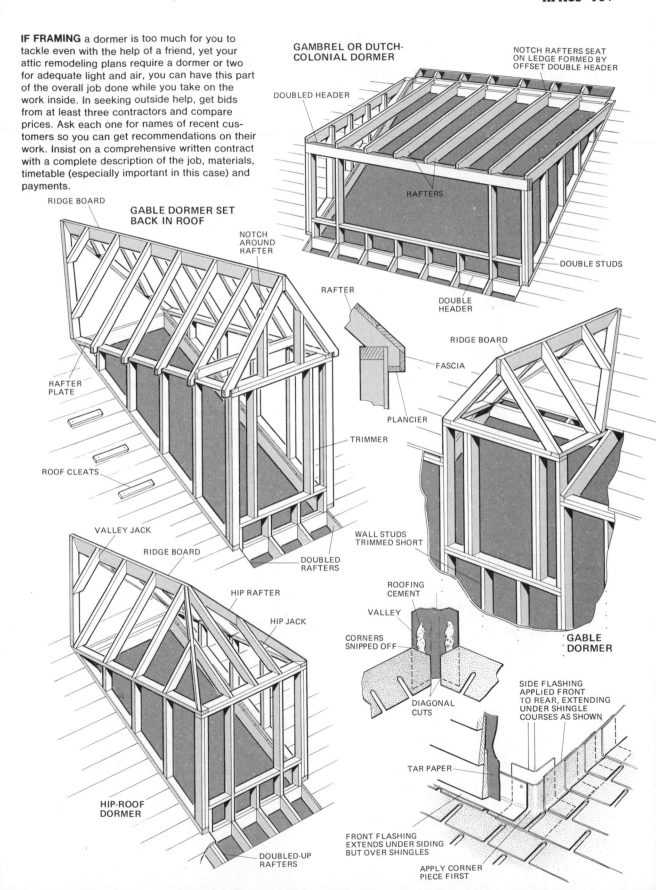

GAMBREL OR DUTCH-COLONIAL DORMER

NOTCH RAFTERS SEAT ON LEDGE FORMED BY OFFSET DOUBLE HEADER

DOUBLED HEADER

RAFTERS

DOUBLE STUDS

DOUBLE HEADER

GABLE DORMER SET BACK IN ROOF

RIDGE BOARD

NOTCH AROUND RAFTER

RAFTER

RIDGE BOARD

FASCIA

PLANCIER

RAFTER PLATE

TRIMMER

ROOF CLEATS

WALL STUDS TRIMMED SHORT

GABLE DORMER

VALLEY JACK

RIDGE BOARD

HIP RAFTER

HIP JACK

DOUBLED RAFTERS

ROOFING CEMENT

VALLEY

CORNERS SNIPPED OFF

DIAGONAL CUTS

SIDE FLASHING APPLIED FRONT TO REAR, EXTENDING UNDER SHINGLE COURSES AS SHOWN

TAR PAPER

HIP-ROOF DORMER

DOUBLED-UP RAFTERS

FRONT FLASHING EXTENDS UNDER SIDING BUT OVER SHINGLES

APPLY CORNER PIECE FIRST

are with hammer and saw and in knowing your limitations. With the exception of a large Dutch colonial dormer, the framing of a single-window dormer isn't as difficult as you may think. Weather is a primary concern. Since you must cut an opening in the roof, you'll need clear weather for at least a couple of days. But be prepared for rain with a tarp you can tuck underneath the shingles and weight it down with a sandbag or two.

The four basic types of dormers are shown here. Select the one that best complements the style of your house. Most important is to have it conform to local building codes.

First lay out the dormer location carefully, then pry up the shingles within the area and about a foot beyond on all sides. Trim back the roofing paper to within a few inches of the shingle line. Before doing any cutting, double the rafters that will frame the opening, cutting the new rafters so they'll extend at least 3 or 4 feet beyond the top and bottom of the hole Then saw the roof boards along the inside of the doubled rafters, and across the top and bottom of the marked opening. The trimmed boards above and below will support the cut rafters until you can spike double headers. Note that the opening should extend one roof-board width past the marked-out area at top and bottom.

The lower edge of the upper double header should be located at ceiling height. The bottom header members have their top edges set flush, at a height that will put the sill 28 to 30 in. above the floor.

Frame the front first

Whenever possible, the side walls of the dormer should be erected over the doubled rafter—on sole plates nailed through the roof boards and into rafters below, using 20-penny (20d) nails. Build the front frame first and nail it in place, bracing it plumb until the rafter plates are in position. Then add the side studs, spacing them 16 in. o.c., driving 16d nails down into them through the rafter plates, and toenailing their lower end to the sole plate with 10d nails.

Next, cut out one end of a 1x6 ridge board to match the roof slope, leaving it overlong; level it by tacking it to a temporary prop standing on the header above the sash opening. Now, lay out and cut a master rafter and use this as a cutting pattern for all dormer rafters except the valley jacks.

Since spans are short in dormer construction, light framing stock is often selected. It isn't unusual for dormers to be framed with 2x4s (or even 2x3s).

Nail the rafters in place with 10d nails, starting from the outer end; then trim the ridge board flush with the outer rafters. A shed-type dormer, such as the gambrel shown, avoids all ridge-board fitting.

The rough window opening is centered in the front frame and should be 4¼ in. wider than the sash unit you select. Whether the trimmer studs are single or double depends on their proximity to the corner posts. When they're close, double trimmers aren't needed. The fourth detail shows a flush-with-wall dormer where the corner posts are merely nailed to existing studs to extend a section of the wall upward; in this case, the rough framing of the window calls for double trimmers.

How a cornice turns corners

The front cornice construction depends on which type of side cornice you choose. In any case, the roof boards run only to the inside face of the front rafter, where they are nailed to a 2x2 cleat fastened along the upper inside edge of the rafter itself, to create the front overhang. In plain cornice construction, this overhang is braced by trim, but for the box type you extend the plancier (or soffit board) its own width beyond the front rafter so you can "turn the corner" with it, nailing the front plancier to a second cleat fastened along the lower front edge of the rafter. Though sketches show the roof boards beveled flush with the side fascia or sheathing, they may project an inch or so if you prefer an overhang effect.

Before shingling, lay a 14-in. sheet-metal valley where dormer and house roof meet, bending it until it lies flat against both roofs. Snap chalk lines up the valley to indicate where shingles must be trimmed. The top corners are also snipped off to shed water toward the valley. To avoid nailing through the valley, anchor the diagonally cut edges of the shingles with cement.

Where the dormer walls meet the roof, use step flashing, starting with a corner piece and working back each side. The side piece should be 6 in. long, with the vertical flange extending at least 3 in. up under the siding and the other flange 4 in. out under the shingles. Don't nail the shingles through the flashing. The front strip rides on top of the shingles.

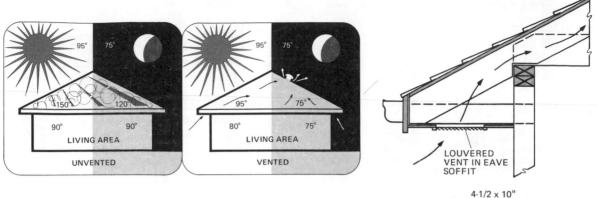

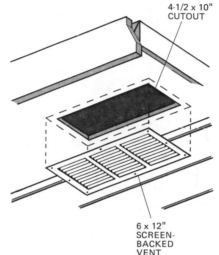

LOUVERED
VENT IN EAVE
SOFFIT

4-1/2 x 10"
CUTOUT

6 x 12"
SCREEN-
BACKED
VENT

Cool your attic to cool your house

■ YOU'VE HEARD of a speed trap; what about a heat trap? Chances are, you have one under your roof.

Step into your attic on a sweltering day. You won't stay long: It's like entering an oven. When super-heated air is trapped in the attic of your home, the temperature is often as much as 60° F. higher than outside. When daytime temperatures reach 95°, it can be as much as 150° in the attic. When the sun goes down, the outside temperature may drop 10° or more. Inside, however, the house continues to stay miserably hot because your attic "oven" is still at work. It takes about eight hours for the attic air to cool down to match the night air. And then, before you know it, the sun is up again and the house begins heating.

The solution, of course, is not to let the heat build up but to replace it throughout the day with fresh cooler air from the outside. When attic temperature is kept low, heat can't radiate to rooms below. Consequently, it takes less cooling to keep your home comfortable on hot days and

nights and, in turn, costs less to cool it since your airconditioning system runs less. Even without airconditioning, you'll feel the difference.

To lower attic temperature significantly it takes more than the small gravity-type vents normally found in roof or gable. On hot days, such stationary ventilators cannot by gravity alone remove heat fast enough to prevent temperature buildup. It takes an automatic exhaust fan—power or wind-driven.

Fans that are automatic and have built-in thermostats start by themselves at a preset temperature. When attic temperature reaches 90°, for example, the fan is set to turn on and run throughout the heat of the day, pulling cooler air in and forcing hot air out. The fan runs until the temperature is below 90°, then shuts off automatically.

Flushing excess heat from your attic is accomplished best when there is an adequate number of air intakes along the eaves. With the fan located at the highest point in the attic and the intake

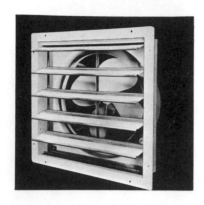

AUTOMATIC 16-in. fan is designed to mount in gable opening. It gives a complete air change every five minutes in an 8500-cu.-ft. attic.

INSTALLING A power vent fan in the gable end of a house requires cutting a suitable opening for it, framing with short 2 x 4 studs and headers and lining with a frame of ¾-in. stock and 1⅛-in. casing. Exterior cover is carefully cut to fit snugly against the casing of frame, then caulked. Dimensions here are for a 16-in. fan that has louvers that seal opening when the fan is off. Bead of caulking is also applied to flange of ventilator when fastening to casing with screws. Fan pulls air through louvers in opposite gable to flush the heat from one end to the other.

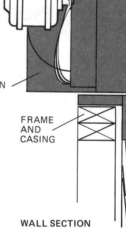

vents at the lowest, uniform air flow is assured. Screenbacked vents (8 x 16 in.) are easy to install in the roof's soffit, but where the roof has no overhang, gable louvers must provide air intake. Ideally, through-the-wall intakes would also be installed in the gables at the attic floor line.

Your home will have a lot to do with the type of exhaust fan you install. So you should take a good look at your house before you make a purchase. If it has a conventional-pitch roof, you have a choice of installing a fan that mounts flush in a gable or one that mounts on the roof. If it has a hip roof, and no gables, the fan will have to be one that's designed to mount in the roof.

Fans for moving air out of the attic are of two types—wind-driven and power fans. The one you choose will depend on how much air you need to move and the cost of energy in your area.

An efficient attic-cooling device, the wind-driven ventilator is gaining acceptance in many energy-short areas of the country. Since it is powered by the wind, it uses no electricity. By cooling the attic continually, it eliminates oven-like heat which, in turn, saves on airconditioning.

Since a wind-driven ventilator is turned by the slightest breeze, it keeps attic air moving, preventing a heat buildup that often reaches temperatures up to 140-150° F. In a well-ventilated attic, less heat is absorbed by the insulation and there's less to radiate down through the ceilings.

Even when there's no wind, a turbine ventilator continues to draw out the heat. Air drawn in through attic vents and escaping through the ventilator causes the unit to turn.

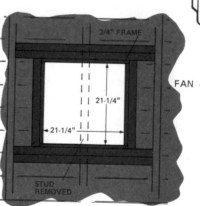

OPENING (REAR VIEW)

WALL SECTION

As a rule of thumb, one 12-in. ventilator is recommended for each 1000 sq. ft. of attic space; two units are best for 1200 sq. ft.

The photos on these pages show how easy it is to install wind-powered ventilators.

Power ventilators

Power ventilators do a more efficient job of cooling than the wind-driven models because

INSTALLING A WIND-DRIVEN OR POWER VENTILATOR

Wind-driven turbine (left) turns with slightest breeze, and escaping attic heat turns it when there is no breeze. Power vent (below, left) is a low-profile ventilator designed for mounting on a roof. It has a 14-in. fan, turns on and shuts off automatically, and works best when intakes are around eaves.

1. LOCATE VENTILATOR from inside attic and at least 24 in. below ridge on rear side of roof.

2. CENTER BASE over pilot hole in roof and use inside of the base to scribe a hole in roof shingles.

they use electricity to move the hot air out and the cooler air in. Power ventilators are thermostatically controlled. Set to turn on automatically when the attic temperature reaches 110° F., the fan will run until the temperature is reduced to approximately 96° F. A cool attic means a cooler house day and night, and it is claimed that the lower room temperature will reduce airconditioning load as much as 30 percent.

Not only will a power ventilator keep your house cooler but it will reduce the possibility of spontaneous combustion in the attic. It will also prevent excessive heat and moisture from deteriorating attic insulation and the shingles.

As for power ventilators, two types are available. The larger, more powerful fans are designed to be mounted in a gable end of the house. Whether you can use this type will depend on the shape and construction of your home. The other type of power ventilator is a smaller, circular fan and is designed to be mounted directly in the roof.

The gable-mounted fans give a complete air change every five minutes when installed in an 8500-cu.-ft. attic. To install this model, you will have to cut an opening in the gable end of the house. This involves removing one of the existing studs, then building in a frame of 2 x 4 studs and headers. This frame should be lined and a casing built per the manufacturer's supplied dimensions. It is important to caulk carefully around

the entire opening to prevent air leaks. Sufficient air intakes should be provided, especially around the eaves, so that the fan is not laboring to keep the air moving.

If a roof-mounted fan is better suited to your house, you can count on one ventilator adequately cooling a home with up to 2000 sq. ft. of living space. Its 14-in. fan does the best job when the attic has at least 300 sq. in. of air intake located along the eaves.

The fan is enclosed in a housing of a durable space-age plastic material that will outlast sheet metal and never need painting. The ventilator measures 27½ in. sq., has a dome 8½ in. high and is operated by a 1/10-hp, 115-v. motor.

The unit should be mounted close to the center of the roof and near the roof ridgeline. Keep in mind that for a neat-looking installation, the unit should be visible only from one side of the roof. This will require the unit to be moved down from the ridge line until it can't be seen from the street.

Installation of a roof-mounted power-ventilator is almost identical to installation of a wind-powered ventilator. The first step is to locate the fan. This should be done from the inside of the attic. By working from the inside you will be able to locate the unit between the roof rafters. When you have determined the best spot, drill a hole up through the roof with an electric drill.

Then go outside and locate the hole. If you have trouble locating the spot, have someone

3. USING CIRCLE as a guide, cut away shingles with a sharp knife. Cut ½ in. outside the circle.

4. CUT HOLE through roof boards with a sabre saw or by hand with a keyhole saw, following the circle.

5. WITH SCREWDRIVER, loosen the locking screw on adjustable-pitch base so you can turn it.

6. WHEN LOOSE, grip top section and turn sufficiently to make the top of the base level.

7. RETIGHTEN SCREW, then slide the top half of flashing up under shingles, removing nails in the way.

8. SECURE BASE to roof with eight roofing nails driven through the flange, then caulk the heads.

9. PLACE VENTILATOR over crimped base; check installation by placing level across the top.

10. USE BASE-RING holes as guide in drilling matching holes around and through the base flange.

11. LOCK RING to flange with No. 8, ½-in. sheet-metal screws. Drive screws home for tight fit.

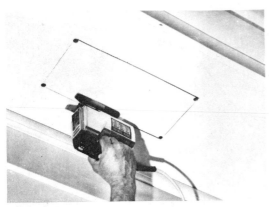

UNLESS you have adequate air intake through which cooler air can be pulled as hot air is exhausted, you can't expect maximum efficiency from your ventilator. Holes are cut in soffit and then capped with louvered cornice vents.

AFTER WIRING, check the proper operation of a powered ventilator with a 60-w. bulb. On a cool day the fan should come on when heated by the bulb and cycle off when the bulb is removed.

shine a flashlight through the hole from inside the attic.

Using the hole as a reference point, draw a 27⅜-in. square outline on the shingles with a crayon or piece of chalk. This will be used to locate the metal base of the unit.

You are now ready to cut the hole. Begin by fashioning a wood compass from a lumber scrap. Drive a nail through one end and drill a hole 17-⅜ inches away to take a crayon for marking. Place the nail in the hole in the roof and carefully scribe a circle on the shingles.

Next, cut through the shingles along the scribe line. This can be done using tin shears or a sharp knife. Clear out the shingles from inside the circle and remove any roofing nails.

Adjust the compass to draw a 15-in.-diameter hole and draw a second hole inside the cleared area. The 15-in. hole is cut through the roofing boards using a sabre saw or keyhole saw. Start in the center where the hole was drilled and work your way to the outside.

You are now ready to install the ventilator. With the unit parallel to the ridgeline of the roof, slide the plastic flange up under the shingles, starting at the center of the hole. Position the unit squarely with the 27⅜-in. outline you marked on the roof. Align the unit with the shingle lines. Continue to slide the flange under the shingles until the round housing can be centered and placed in the hole. You may have to go inside the attic to verify that the unit is properly positioned.

Nail the exposed portion of the flange to the roof. Galvanized roofing nails should be used to prevent rust. Check the unit for leakage using a garden hose. Because of the way the fan is positioned under the shingles, it should not leak. If it does, use butyl rubber caulking along the edges of the flange.

Electrical installation

The control box for the unit should be screwed to an attic rafter. When connecting to the 110-v. line, follow the wiring diagram furnished by the manufacturer. All wiring should meet local building codes. If you have questions about proper installation, consult an electrician.

You are now ready to verify proper operation of the unit. The checkout procedure can be used for both roof and gable-mounted models. Put a 60-w. bulb in a drop cord. Turn on the current to the fan on a day when the attic is cool. The fan should not start. By bringing the bulb near the thermostat in the control box, you should be able to get the fan to start operating. If not, check all electrical connections carefully. Likewise, the fan should shut off when the bulb is removed from the vicinity of the control box.

When to install

The best time to install any attic ventilation device is in the spring. There is nothing worse than prowling around in an overheated attic to connect a fan and verify its operation. And by installing it before you need it, you will reduce your airconditioning bills and keep your house comfortable all summer.

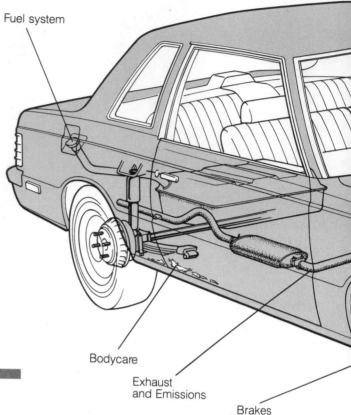

Fuel system

Bodycare

Exhaust
and Emissions

Brakes

Automobile maintenance and care

■ GOOD CAR CARE is simply a matter of determining the useful life of normal maintenance items and replacing them before they fail, or before they have a negative effect on other parts. Car care is not a plan for saving an old, neglected vehicle. Good car care should start the day your automobile rolls off the showroom floor. It is worth some effort to know the basic systems that make a car run. Then you can identify and correct problems before they become costly and possibly dangerous.

Your car has a variety of systems, each with many operating parts. Through normal use, many of the 15,000 parts in your car gradually deteriorate. Some wear out sooner than others because they work harder. Many can last the life of your car. The performance of each system depends not only on the condition of all its own parts, but also on the proper operation of other related systems.

ENGINE PERFORMANCE
Your car's engine

The internal-combustion engine in your car converts fuel and air to power. When you step on the gas pedal and turn the key in the ignition, you set off a chain of events that make the internal-combustion engine work. The accelerator is part of the fuel system that sends a mixture of fuel and air to the cylinders to burn. In a gasoline engine, the ignition switch is part of the electrical system that controls the spark used to ignite the mixture, causing combustion inside the cylinder (internal combustion). Diesels use the heat of the com-

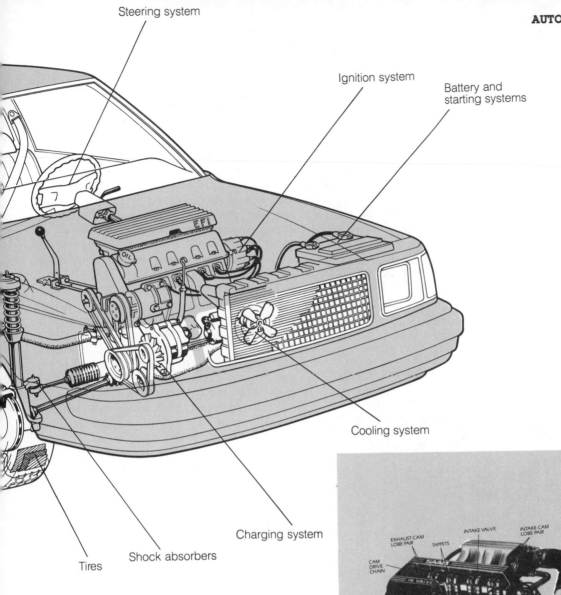

Steering system

Ignition system

Battery and starting systems

Cooling system

Charging system

Shock absorbers

Tires

pressed gases in the cylinder to ignite the mixture.

The expansion of the burning fuel inside the cylinders pushes the *piston* down, turning the crankshaft through *connecting rods.* The *crankshaft* changes the up and down motion of the pistons into the turning motion of the drive line. The *flywheel,* attached to the crankshaft, is a heavy disk whose momentum keeps the crankshaft turning when the pistons are between power strokes. The *valve train* is a precisely timed mechanism used to open and close the intake and exhaust valves at the top of the cylinders in synchronization with the movement of the pistons. The valve train governs the inflow of fuel and air and the outflow of waste gases (from the exhaust).

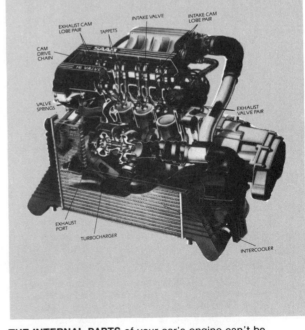

THE INTERNAL PARTS of your car's engine can't be inspected easily, so you have to rely on performance to tell you when something is about to go wrong.

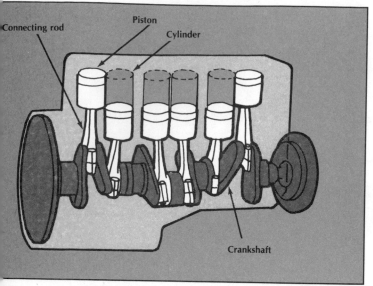

THE INTERNAL-COMBUSTION engine burns fuel inside the cylinders. Expansion of the burning fuel pushes the pistons down in the cylinders, turning the crankshaft and flywheel through the connecting rods.

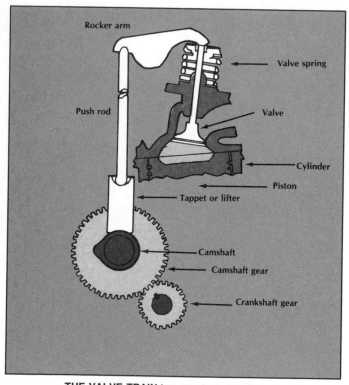

THE VALVE TRAIN is a precisely timed mechanism that opens and closes the intake and exhaust valves in time with the movement of the pistons. It controls the inflow of air and fuel and the outflow of waste gases.

Engine performance diagnosis

You cannot easily inspect the internal parts of your car's engine to tell when they begin to wear or break down. You have to rely on other signs in the performance of your car to tell you when something inside the engine isn't right. Finding the cause of a problem before it gets serious will help you prolong the life of your engine.

You can usually determine the source of engine performance problems by a logical troubleshooting procedure. Unfortunately, that can require expensive equipment, including a voltmeter, oscilloscope, vacuum gauge, power balance tester, tachometer, emissions analyzer, compression gauge and cylinder leakage tester.

A knowledgeable do-it-yourselfer can sometimes arrive at a diagnosis with only a vacuum gauge and compression gauge, particularly if an internal engine problem is the source of a driveability complaint. On older vehicles without electronic ignition or catalytic converters, you can perform a power balance test by removing plug cables one at a time with insulated pliers, while noting engine speed change on a tachometer. (The speed drop for each cylinder should be within 5 percent of the others if the engine is operating efficiently.) In most cases, however, the experience and equipment of a skilled professional will be needed to uncover specific fuel, ignition or emission component faults.

There are many excellent diagnostic tools you can buy to help track down a problem with your car. But if you learn how to use your ears and nose, they can be among the best tools you have. Interpreting car noises and odors can be tricky. It requires not only a sharp sense of hearing and smell, but also some practice.

Procedures for engine performance improvement

Our do-it-yourself guide for **Engine Performance** maintenance is in Volume 9. There you'll find a basic course in engine tune-up followed by tips on how to diagnose engine noise. Also included in the section is help in curing missing, surging and lack of power in your car, stalling problems, and tracking down the causes of engine misfire.

STARTING SYSTEM

What your car's starting system does

The purpose of the starting or cranking system is to get the engine turning so it can begin run-

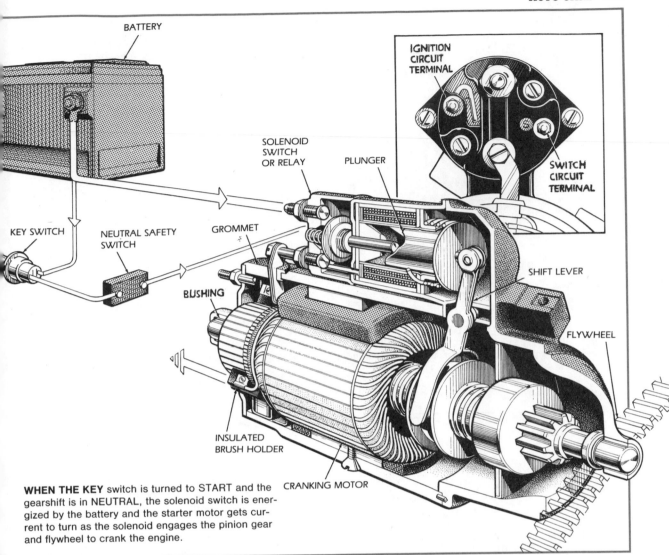

BATTERY

IGNITION
CIRCUIT
TERMINAL

SOLENOID
SWITCH
OR RELAY

PLUNGER

SWITCH
CIRCUIT
TERMINAL

KEY SWITCH

NEUTRAL SAFETY
SWITCH

GROMMET

SHIFT LEVER

BUSHING

FLYWHEEL

INSULATED
BRUSH HOLDER

CRANKING MOTOR

WHEN THE KEY switch is turned to START and the gearshift is in NEUTRAL, the solenoid switch is energized by the battery and the starter motor gets current to turn as the solenoid engages the pinion gear and flywheel to crank the engine.

ning on its own. When the car key activates the *ignition switch,* it starts the flow of electricity from the battery to the cranking and charging systems as well as to car accessories. The *neutral safety switch* prevents cranking the engine when the transmission is in gear. The *battery* converts chemical energy into electrical energy needed when the charging system isn't supplying energy from the alternator. The *starter relay* is an electromagnetic switch connecting the battery to the starter motor. The *starter solenoid* is an electromechanical switch on the starter. It engages the gear on the starter motor shaft with the ring gear on the flywheel. The *starter motor* is a small, powerful electric motor designed to crank the engine by turning the flywheel through a ring gear arrangement.

Starting system maintenance

Proper battery service and maintenance can solve most problems with your car's starting system. Inspect the battery, cables and surrounding areas for signs of corrosion, loose or broken carriers, cracked or bulged cases, dirt or acid. The battery hold-down bolts should be properly tightened. Keep the top of the battery clean of acid film and dirt because this kind of contamination can create current flow between the terminals and slowly discharge the battery.

For best results in cleaning a battery, first wash it with a diluted ammonia or baking soda solution to neutralize any acid present. Then flush off with clean water. Keep the vent plugs tight and plug the vent holes with toothpicks so the neutralizing solution does not enter the cells. After cleaning, apply a coat of petroleum jelly to the battery hold-down bolts and cable clamps. The hold-down bolts should be kept tight enough to prevent the battery from shaking around in its carrier, but they should not be tightened to the

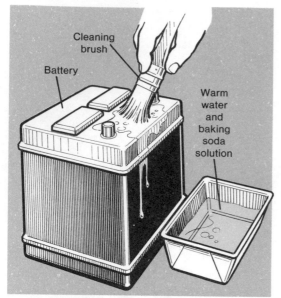

PREVENT BATTERY CORROSION by periodic cleaning with baking soda solution. Cover vent holes to keep cleaning solution out of the battery. Be careful of any spilled acid from the battery.

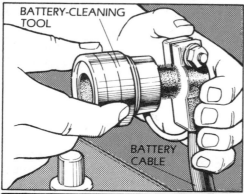

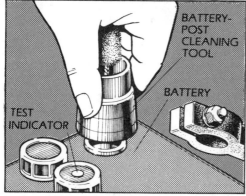

CLEAN ANY CORROSION off the terminals and cable ends with special cleaning brushes. A light coating of petroleum jelly on the outside of the terminals will help prevent corrosion from happening again.

point where the battery is placed under a strain.

To ensure good contact, the battery cables should be tight on the battery posts. If the battery posts or cable terminals are corroded, remove the cables and clean them with baking soda solution and a wire brush. Be careful when working around the battery: Do not smoke, and avoid sparks and open flames. The electrolyte in the battery gives off highly explosive hydrogen gas.

Procedures for starting system maintenance

Our do-it-yourself guide for periodic maintenance on the **Battery and Starting System** parts is in Volume 2. This section begins with help for troubleshooting starting system problems. Specific do-it-yourself instructions on taking care of maintenance-free batteries is followed by plans to build a meter to prevent you from electrocuting your car's battery.

CHARGING SYSTEM

What your car's charging system does

The charging system keeps the battery fully charged and provides the power for the car's electrical systems.

The *alternator* supplies the electrical needs. It is driven by a belt from a pulley on the crankshaft and produces electricity for other electrical systems and for the car's accessories. The *voltage regulator* controls the electrical output of the alternator. It's under the hood (on the cowl, inner-fender pan or radiator support). In some cars, the voltage regulator is built into the alternator unit itself.

Charging system maintenance

There's practically no maintenance required for the charging system. General troubleshooting procedures consist of a glance at the warning light or gauge on the instrument panel. This will usually tell you when the system is not putting out enough power. Even if the light or gauge isn't working, the battery will serve as a warning. It will soon discharge if the charging system fails.

One condition you have to watch for is failure of the voltage regulator to limit alternator output. Without regulation, an alternator will overcharge the battery and ruin components that use electricity. For instance, bulbs and fuses that can't handle excessive current will burn out. Battery electrolyte (sulfuric acid) will vaporize quickly if too much charging current is supplied. Unless you spot the depleting electrolyte supply soon

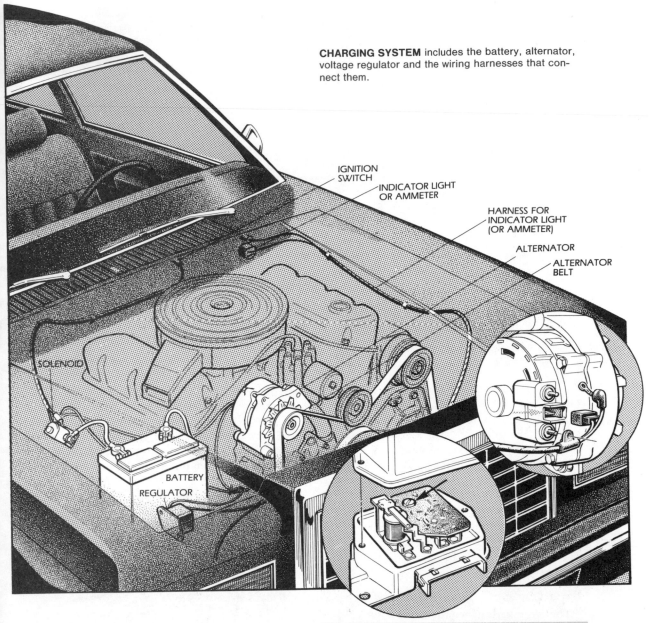

CHARGING SYSTEM includes the battery, alternator, voltage regulator and the wiring harnesses that connect them.

IGNITION SWITCH

INDICATOR LIGHT OR AMMETER

HARNESS FOR INDICATOR LIGHT (OR AMMETER)

ALTERNATOR

ALTERNATOR BELT

SOLENOID

BATTERY

REGULATOR

enough, dry plates will deteriorate and the battery will die. An overcharged battery can even explode if the excess hydrogen gas comes near a spark.

If the battery electrolyte is frequently low, the system is probably overcharging. If you don't check the electrolyte level, you may get whiffs of the gas; it smells like rotten eggs. If your car has a voltmeter or ammeter, you can easily spot an overcharging condition. If battery voltage frequently is over 14.5 volts, or if an ammeter shows continuous high charge rates, overcharging is likely, and a basic charging system diagnostic test should be performed.

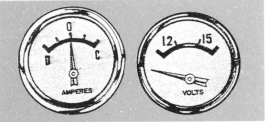

THE AMMETER (left) indicates the flow of current into (charge) or out of (discharge) the battery. The voltmeter (right) will indicate the higher voltage present when the battery is being charged. If the battery becomes discharged, the reduced voltage will be apparent on the meter.

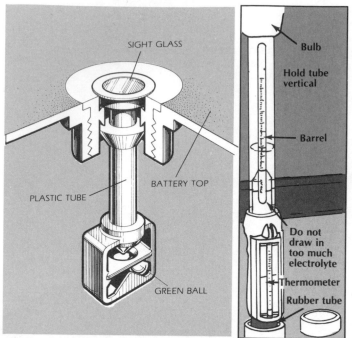

SIGHT GLASS

PLASTIC TUBE

BATTERY TOP

GREEN BALL

Bulb

Hold tube vertical

Barrel

Do not draw in too much electrolyte

Thermometer

Rubber tube

Take reading at eye level

Ignore slight curvature

If your hydrometer does not adjust for temperature, add .004 points to your reading for each 10° above 80°F. For each 10° below 80°F subtract .004 points

Percentage-of-Charge Table		
State of charge	Standard specific gravity as used in temperate climates	Speci gravit built water
Fully charged	1.280	
75% charged	1.250	
50% charged	1.220	
25% charged	1.190	
Discharged	1.130	

MAINTENANCE-FREE batteries indicate state-of-charge with built-in hydrometers.

A HYDROMETER IS used to check the battery's acid-and-water mixture, indicating its state-of-charge.

Procedures for charging system checks

Detailed procedures for doing a basic charging system diagnostic test begin our do-it-yourself section on the **Charging System** in Volume 5. This is followed by instructions for checking and adjusting drive belt tension, one of the primary causes of failure in the charging system. In Volume 5 you will also find an explanation of underhood wiring and step-by-step instructions for checking your alternator.

IGNITION SYSTEM

What your car's ignition system does

The ignition system produces a high voltage and delivers it to the spark plugs at a precise instant to ignite the compressed mixture of fuel and air in the cylinders. The system has a primary and secondary circuit, and switching is done electronically or through the older breaker-point system.

Breaker-point ignition. In the older breaker-point ignition systems, the points and condenser are in the distributor. The *points* are an electrical switch to open or close the primary circuit. The opening action of the points builds up the high voltage in the secondary circuit needed for a spark at the spark plugs. When the *distributor cam* turns and a lobe comes in contact with the

rubbing block of the points, it pushes the points open. A spring closes the points, completing the circuit as the cam turns and the lobe moves off the rubbing block. In the distributor, the *rotor* is keyed to the cam in such a way that it is in a po-

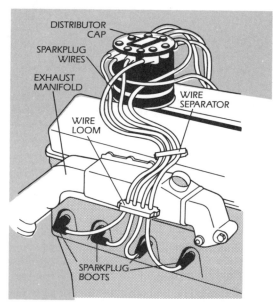

DISTRIBUTOR CAP

SPARKPLUG WIRES

EXHAUST MANIFOLD

WIRE SEPARATOR

WIRE LOOM

SPARKPLUG BOOTS

THE JOB OF THE ignition system is to get a high-voltage spark to each spark plug just when it is needed to ignite the mixture in that cylinder.

sition to transfer the high voltage from the *coil* to the distributor cap towers when the points begin to open. The *distributor cap* provides a separate path for high voltage from the coil through the rotor to each of the towers on the cap. The spark plug cables carry the high voltage from the towers to the *spark plugs.*

Electronic ignition. One major difficulty with the breaker-point ignition system is its inability to maintain constant ignition timing because the contacts wear changing the point gap. This problem has been solved with electronic ignition. An electronic ignition system has a magnetic *pickup* assembly to send signals to an electronic control module. A *reluctor* in the electronic system replaces the cam, and a magnetic pickup assembly replaces the points. The rotating reluctor never touches the magnetic pickup, so they don't wear. The pickup assembly sends an electrical signal to the *electronic control module,* where a transistor (an electronic switch with no moving parts) makes and breaks the primary circuit, allowing the ignition coil to produce a high or secondary voltage—as high as 40,000 volts in many systems. In most cars, all other ignition components—the mechanical advance unit, vacuum advance unit, rotor, and distributor cap and spark plugs— function the same as in the breaker-point system.

Ignition system maintenance

Ignition system maintenance begins by removing and inspecting the spark plugs. Be careful when removing spark plug cables. Don't pull on the cable. Grasp the rubber boot that fits over the plug and twist it back and forth a bit until it loosens its grip on the plug. Then pull the cable off while twisting the boot. Once the plugs have been removed, you can inspect their electrodes. They should be light to medium white, brown or gray. If they are coated with wet fuel and oil, sooty black carbon or grease, or heavy black deposits, a diagnostic check is necessary to determine the cause of plug fouling. On cars with electronic ignition, if the plugs look good and they're only 15,000 miles old, you can clean and gap them and put them back for another 15,000. With breaker-point ignitions, replacement is best even if the plugs look fairly good.

Next, turn your attention to the distributor. Remove the cap and clean the inside with a clean rag. Check for fractures, cracks or evidence of carbon tracks on the surface of the cap. Replace the cap if any of these conditions exists. Clean the terminals inside the cap with a small knife. If corrosion cannot be easily scraped from the ter-

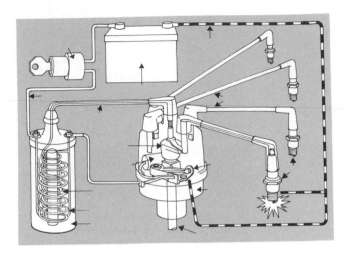

THE PRIMARY CIRCUIT has the battery, ignition switch, coil, points and condenser. The low voltage in this circuit generates a high voltage in the *secondary circuit,* which contains the coil, distributor, spark plug wires and spark plugs.

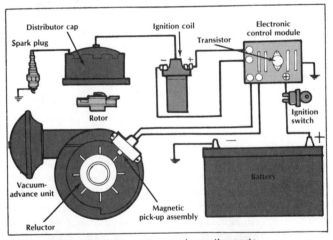

AN ELECTRONIC ignition system replaces the parts that wear with electronic circuits, which not only increases the life of the ignition parts but gives more precise control for more efficient and emission-free operation of your car.

minals, replace the cap. Pull the rotor from the distributor and examine it carefully. It should also be replaced if it is fractured, chipped or carbon-tracked or if the tip is corroded or burned to the point where it can't be cleaned without removing metal.

If your car has a breaker-point ignition, turn the engine until the rubbing block is on the high point of the distributor cam. Unhook the primary

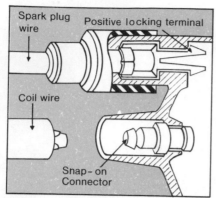

SOME DISTRIBUTORS have locking spark plug wires that must be removed from inside the cap. Press the hook-spring clips together with long-nose pliers and push the wire out from inside the cap.

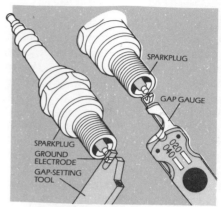

CHECK SPARK PLUG gap with a wire gauge. Adjust by bending the ground electrode with a special tool.

lead and condenser wire from the points. Then remove the points and condenser, taking care not to lose any screws. (On many cars, the screws need only to be loosened to remove the contact points.) Install new points and condenser, then adjust the point gap to the car maker's specifications, using a feeler gauge. Lubricate the breaker cam with a very light coating of cam lubricant or white lithium grease. Don't overdo it. Reassemble the distributor, start the engine and check the point adjustment with a dwell meter if you have one.

If your car has electronic ignition, there is no specific interval for replacement of the control module and pickup, although the cap and rotor may wear out faster than they do in contact point distributors. Electronic pickup devices and control modules do fail, but they do not wear out at a certain mileage. You must do a fault-finding diagnostic routine to pinpoint the fault when they fail. Handheld electronic ignition testers are now available at a relatively low price. These instruments check whether the pickup is producing a signal for the control module, and then test the control module by providing a simulated pickup signal.

Before reinstalling the cap and rotor, check the centrifugal advance mechanism if your car has one (the latest cars have fully electronic timing control).

When the engine has warmed, adjust idle speed to spec and set ignition timing with a timing light or meter. Once the initial spark timing has been adjusted, check the vacuum advance (if used) by disconnecting the hose, accelerating the engine to 1500 rpm, then reconnecting it to see if the engine timing advances. To check centrifugal advance, accelerate the engine to 3500 rpm while watching the timing marks with your light or timing meter. Electronic advance mechanisms should also adjust timing as the engine is accelerated.

Procedures for ignition system adjustments

Do-it-yourself procedures for **Ignition Systems** are in Volume 14. There you'll find help to troubleshoot and adjust both electronic ignitions and the older point-type systems. You'll also find a do-it-yourself guide for distributor tune-up and a helpful article on how to read your spark plugs to diagnose ignition or engine problems in your car.

CURB-IDLE SPEED is set with the engine warm and the choke fully open. Turn the idle-speed adjusting screw on the carburetor clockwise to increase idle speed, counterclockwise to decrease it.

LUBRICATION SYSTEM

What your car's lubrication system does

The lubricating oil in the engine has five major functions: (1) It reduces friction by lubricating moving parts, minimizing power loss. (2) It helps in cooling by flowing between the internal parts carrying much of the destructive heat away. (3) It cleans by washing away abrasive materials from friction surfaces. (4) It seals by filling gaps between the moving parts such as the pistons, rings and cylinders. (5) It absorbs shock between bearings and other parts, reducing engine noise and extending engine life.

Oil change and lubrication

Nine out of 10 professional mechanics will tell you that the best thing you can do for your car is to change the oil and filter frequently. A good supply of fresh, clean motor oil in the crankcase will prevent the kind of metal wear that can make your car old before its time.

An interval of 3,000 miles will provide maximum protection in most cases. Car makers' suggested intervals are, of course, much longer—as long as 15,000 miles in some cases. If the car makers accept this long interval, you can be sure that a change of oil and filter at 3,000 miles won't hurt.

Warm the engine oil thoroughly by driving at least five miles before you prepare to change the oil and filter. Then raise the car on solid jackstands that are securely located. Raise both the rear and front of the car so oil will drain properly

THE OIL PUMP circulates oil, under pressure, to all internal moving parts. The pump picks up oil from the pan and sends it through a filter for cleaning and through passageways to all moving parts of the engine.

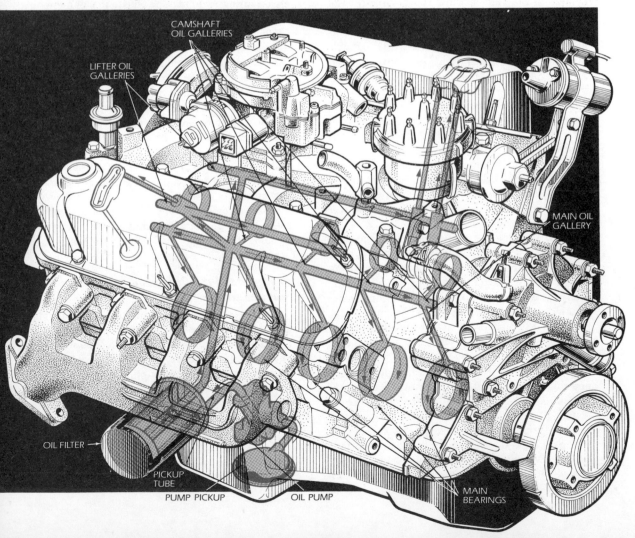

LIFTER OIL GALLERIES

CAMSHAFT OIL GALLERIES

MAIN OIL GALLERY

OIL FILTER →

PICKUP TUBE

PUMP PICKUP

OIL PUMP

MAIN BEARINGS

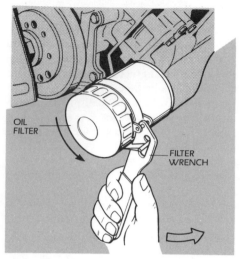

A BAND-TYPE oil filter wrench grips securely to make removal clean and simple.

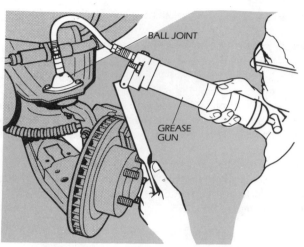

SNAP THE COUPLING of the grease gun onto the grease fitting and pump grease in until the dust boot begins to swell or until grease is forced out of the bottom of the joint.

and you can lube the chassis and inspect the underside of the vehicle while you change the oil.

Use a box wrench or socket wrench to remove the oil drain plug. Let the warm oil drain completely. You can change the filter while the oil is draining. Use a filter wrench to remove the old oil filter, making sure the gasket comes off with it. Wipe the filter mounting surface with a clean rag. Partially fill your new filter with some of the oil you're going to use to refill the crankcase. Apply a bit of oil to the filter gasket. Install the filter, tightening it according to the instructions on the filter box. If there are no instructions, tighten it about a three-quarter turn past the point where the gasket first contacts the mount or almost as tight as you can make it by hand. *Don't tighten it past a three-quarter turn.*

When the oil stops draining, replace the plug and tighten it only medium-firm with a wrench that is no more than 10 inches long. Don't overtighten. Refill the crankcase with the oil recommended by the car maker. For most conditions, multigrade oils are preferred. Manufacturers recommend SF oils for the latest gasoline engine cars and SF/CC or SF/CD oils for the latest diesel engines.

Once you fill the engine with the correct amount of oil, start it and let it run for a minute. Check for leaks then shut it off and check the oil level.

Lubricate all steering linkage and suspension fittings with water-resistant EP chassis lubrication every time you change the oil and filter. Check these points for excessive looseness. Lu-bricate the ball joints. If your car does not have grease fittings, you may be able to install them on some parts.

Check the level of the rear axle lube, and add the recommended lubricant if it is low. Usually there's a plug in the side of the differential center section or in the rear cover for you to check this lube level. It should, in most cases, come right up to the hole or to within ¼ inch of the hole.

Before you finish, use engine oil in a small squirt can to lube the accelerator linkage under the hood and the pivot points on the hood hinges and lock mechanism. Check the fluid levels in the power steering reservoir, brake master cylinders and automatic transmission. Check the transaxle lube level on front-wheel-drive cars. In most cases, both automatic and manual transaxles use the same type of ATF as a lubricant. Check your owner's manual.

Procedures for lubrication system maintenance

Complete instructions on how to lubricate your car are in the do-it-yourself section on car **Lubrication Systems** in Volume 15. You will also find a handy reference guide telling you how to diagnose excess oil consumption in your car.

COOLING SYSTEM

What your car's cooling system does

The heat generated in the combustion chamber of an engine's cylinders can be over 4,500 °F. A temperature this high can destroy the engine's lubrication system and its internal moving parts. Approximately one-third of the engine's heat is used to produce power, one-third leaves through the exhaust system, and the remaining one-third must be dissipated through the cooling system. The coolant used in today's engines is a mixture of water and permanent antifreeze (ethylene glycol). This mixture has a lower freezing point and a higher boiling point than water. In today's cars, temperature stability is the key to operating efficiency. These engines are designed to run hotter, but at a more constant temperature than engines made before emissions controls and rigid carburetor and ignition timing requirements.

Cooling system service

Any maintenance plan for your car should include a yearly cooling system inspection and flush as well as new coolant.

The system should be pressurized with a cooling system pressure tester before the inspection begins. To do this, fill the radiator almost to the top with water. Attach the pressure tester to the filler neck of the radiator. Pump the tester up to the pressure rating of the radiator cap. If the system holds pressure, you can assume there are no leaks. If the pressure reading on the gauge gradually falls, there is a leak somewhere in the cooling system. Examine all hose connections, gasket joints, freeze plugs and the water pump shaft seal. Look for coolant leaks wherever there is evidence of core damage on the radiator, or where the tanks are connected to the radiator core. Your mechanic can help you diagnose a leaking head gasket by checking for exhaust emissions at the radiator outlet with the probe of an emissions analyzer while the engine is running.

Once you're sure the system is leak-free, you can flush out the old coolant. A simple cooling system flushing kit is available from auto parts stores. The kit has a tee to install in the heater inlet hose (the hose that's not connected to the water pump). The flushing kit usually comes with a restrictor to install in the radiator neck while the system is being flushed.

Once the flushing kit is installed, turn on the garden hose and let water flow through the cooling system until it runs clean for several minutes. Remove the garden hose, and seal the flushing tee with the cap that comes with the kit. (The tee can be left in place for future service.) Once the flushing is complete, drain the water out of the radiator and coolant recovery tank.

Add new coolant. If your car has any aluminum engine or cooling system parts, you must use

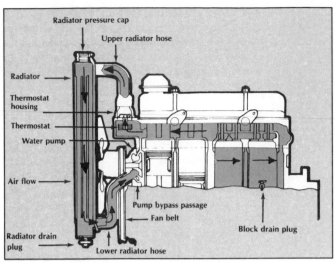

THE WATER PUMP, driven by a belt on the crankshaft pulley, moves the coolant through the engine block, radiator and heater. The coolant absorbs heat from the metal parts of the engine.

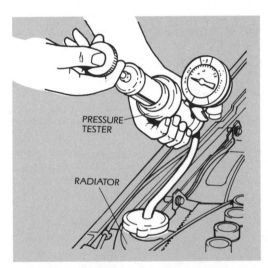

WITH THE RADIATOR pressure-cap adapter connected, pump the test pump until the gauge reads 15 psi. If pressure reading doesn't hold 2 minutes, there is a leak somewhere.

antifreeze that's specially formulated for use in aluminum engines. The coolant should be a mix of at least 50 percent antifreeze combined with water. You can get additional freeze protection by using as much as 70 percent antifreeze, but no more. Freeze protection actually decreases with more than 70 percent ethylene glycol in the coolant.

The radiator usually will hold about half of the coolant; the engine and hoses hold the rest. Once the radiator is filled, run the engine until the level drops, then add some more.

You can also add some coolant to the recovery tank. When you think you've filled the system completely, replace the cap, let the engine run for a while, let it cool down, remove the cap and check the coolant level. Check the level in the recovery tank, too.

Procedures for cooling system maintenance

Our do-it-yourself procedures for maintaining your car's **Cooling System** are in Volume 6. There you'll also find help in locating the causes of overheating and ways to protect your car against the cold. If you have an older car without a coolant recovery system, there are directions in this section of Volume 6 to tell you how to install one.

FUEL SYSTEM

What your car's fuel system does

Your car's fuel system includes a tank to store a supply of fuel that is fed to a carburetor or fuel injection system for vaporization and distribution to the cylinders in the engine.

Carburetion. The carburetor combines gasoline with air into an explosive substance. This mixture of fuel and air is drawn through the intake manifold and valves into the combustion chamber by the downward movement of the piston on the intake stroke. The ideal mixture, or one that burns most efficiently, has about 15 parts of air to one part of gasoline. The carburetor adjusts the mixture of fuel and air to meet different demands of speeds, loads and temperatures.

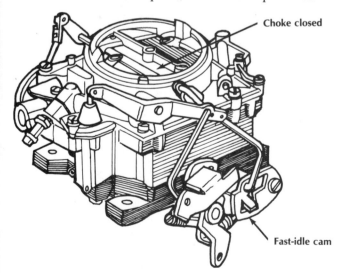

CARBURETOR COMBINES air and gasoline into an explosive mixture and sends it to the cylinders through the intake manifold.

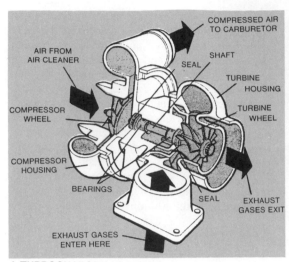

A TURBOCHARGER FORCES air into the engine when the exhaust gases spin a turbine wheel. This increases the power output.

Fuel Injection. In the gasoline fuel-injection system, there is no carburetor. Nozzles spray or inject fuel under high pressure into the airstream being drawn into the combustion chamber. Fuel can be injected continuously into the intake manifold, allowing intake valves to control when it enters the cylinders. It can also be timed to spray intermittently, and each cylinder has its own injector that sprays only at the precise instant with the precise amount of fuel needed for combustion. Fuel injection systems are controlled mechanically or electronically. Mechanical systems use vacuum and airflow signals from the engine to control the mixture of air and fuel injected. Electronically controlled systems use sensors in various parts of the system to signal a small computer or control module. This electronic control module (ECM) determines when the injection of fuel should occur and how much fuel should be injected for the optimum mixture of air and fuel burned in the combustion chamber.

Turbocharging. A turbocharger forces air into the manifold at pressures higher than atmospheric pressure. In a gasoline engine, increasing the manifold pressure to twice the atmospheric pressure can double the power output of the engine. Passenger car boost from a turbo will normally range from about 6 to 12 psi.

Maintaining fuel system components

Precise adjustment of both the curb idle and the air/fuel mixture on a carburetor is essential

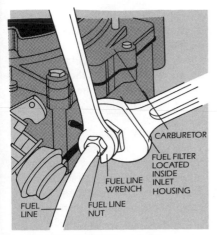

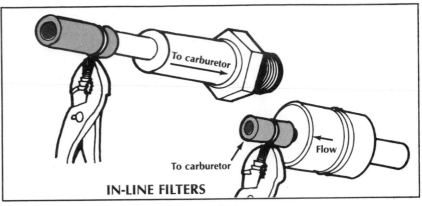

IN-LINE FILTERS

SOME FUEL FILTERS are in the carburetor. When disconnecting the fuel line for service, use two wrenches to prevent damage.

ON CARS WITH in-line fuel filters, remove spring clips or clamps and slide the hoses off to replace the filter.

to the performance of a car engine. Rough idling, poor gas mileage, engine stalling, dieseling and highly polluted exhaust are results of incorrect carburetor adjustment.

On late-model carburetors, the screws used to adjust the air/fuel mixture, located in the base of the carburetor, are set at the factory and sealed with plastic or steel limiter caps to maintain the correct mixture setting necessary to meet emission-control specifications. These limiter caps should not be removed, disturbed or tampered with. If your car has these caps, the only adjustment you can make is curb-idle rpm.

Examine the air filter every time you perform a maintenance tuneup and replace it if it is coated with dirt. Although most manufacturers recommend 30,000-mile replacement, air filters seem to last only about 15,000 miles in typically dirty urban areas, and even less where there is a lot of blowing dust.

Gasoline engine fuel filters should be replaced at 15,000- to 20,000-mile intervals, or once a year, whichever comes first. Don't ignore fuel filters hidden behind the inlet nut on the carburetor, as they are on most Ford and GM cars. Use two wrenches to remove the inlet line: one on the fuel line nut, one on the carb's inlet fitting. Then remove the inlet fitting itself. The filter is behind it. Chrysler products and many imports have fuel filters spliced into the fuel line and held with hose clamps. To remove them, simply loosen the clamps, move them away from the filter and twist the neoprene hoses back and forth to get them off. Some imports have two fuel filters. Cars with

electric fuel pumps often have the pump and filter near the gas tank. Fuel filter service is even more critical on diesel engines. Replace all diesel fuel filters at recommended intervals or 20 to 30 percent sooner.

Turbocharger service is not normally done unless you are sure the problem is in the turbocharger. Many times problems in other parts of the engine are blamed on the turbocharger. For example, a dirty air filter will increase smoking and oil consumption by creating a partial vacuum at the turbo bearings. The turbo could be at fault if there is a lack of power, excessive exhaust smoke, an unusual noise or excessive consumption of oil or fuel. One of the most useful checks of your turbocharger is the sounds from the engine compartment. Any change in noise levels can isolate problems. A higher pitch can indicate an air leak between the air cleaner and the engine, or gases leaking between the engine block and compressor inlet. Noise-level cycling can indicate a plugged air cleaner, restrictions from the air cleaner to the compressor, or heavy dirt buildup in the compressor housing or on the compressor wheel.

Procedures for fuel system adjustments

Our do-it-yourself procedures for adjustments you can make to your car's **Fuel System** are in Volume 10. There you'll find an explanation of what you should know about your fuel system. This is followed by a troubleshooting guide for carburetors and a guide for turbocharger maintenance and repair.

EXHAUST AND EMISSIONS-CONTROL SYSTEMS

What your car's exhaust and emissions-control systems do

The exhaust system gets rid of the burned gases from the engine. Harmful gases, including unburned fuel (hydrocarbons), burned fuel (carbon monoxide) and high combustion temperatures that produce oxides of nitrogen, are emitted by the car and cause pollution. The *charcoal canister* is a container filled with activated charcoal used to trap gasoline vapor before it enters the outside air from the fuel tank and carburetor. The *PCV valve* controls the flow of crankcase vapors, sending them back to the engine to be burned. The *exhaust-gas-recirculation valve* (*EGR*) limits the emission of hydrocarbons. Carbon monoxide is controlled primarily by a well-tuned engine and the higher operating temperature of today's engines. But the hotter temperatures also increase emissions of nitrogen oxides. The three-way *catalytic converter* controls the emission of nitrogen oxides (NOx) by sensing the amount of oxygen in the exhaust and adjusting the carburetor to keep the level within controlled limits.

Exhaust and emissions-control system checks

Check all around the exhaust system components for deterioration or discoloration that could indicate a leak in the system.

The PCV valve filter and hoses should be cleaned every 15,000 miles. The valve and filter should be replaced every 30,000 miles. To check the valve, remove the valve at the intake manifold or rocker arm cover and run the engine at idle. Check for vacuum at the end of the valve with your thumb. If there is no vacuum, check for clogging of the valve or the hoses. Replace any hose that is not in good shape. With the engine off, remove the valve. Shake it and listen for the rattle of the needle inside. If the valve doesn't rattle, it should be replaced.

While you need an exhaust gas analyzer for a full check of the catalytic converter, you can look for physical damage such as large dents, ruptures, punctures or excessive heat discoloration of the converter and scorching of the underbody just above the converter. These conditions can indicate a defective unit. A visual check can, however, be misleading. For example, a poorly tuned engine can cause the converter to overheat and discolor. Only an exhaust-gas analyzer can determine if the converter is defective or if the engine isn't working right.

Procedures for exhaust and emissions-control system service

Specific how-to-do-it help for the **Exhaust and Emission-Control Systems** is in Volume 8. There you are given directions on how to replace your exhaust system and how to check emission controls in general with specific focus on the catalytic converter and the EGR system.

THE DRIVE LINE

What the parts in your car's drive line do

The drive line of your car includes all those parts between the engine flywheel and the wheels. The *transmission* is a box containing the gears. It varies the speed and torque (turning power) of the driving axle in relation to the speed and torque of the engine. Getting the car to move from a complete standstill requires the greatest torque. This is first or low gear. Once the car is underway, less torque is needed to keep it moving. The transmission, therefore, can be shifted into gears giving lower torque and greater speed: second, third, fourth and sometimes fifth gear. There are also two other positions of the transmission: reverse for backing up and neutral for complete disengagement of the engine from the rest of the drive line. The *clutch* assembly used with a manual transmission mechanically engages and disengages the engine from the transmission so the gears can be shifted.

The *automatic transmission,* like the manual transmission, shifts into its various speeds to provide a smooth transmission of torque and speed from the engine to the driveshaft. The automatic

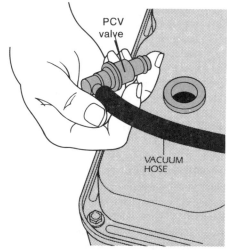

PCV valve

VACUUM HOSE

WITH THE ENGINE running, check PCV system by feeling for vacuum at the end of the valve.

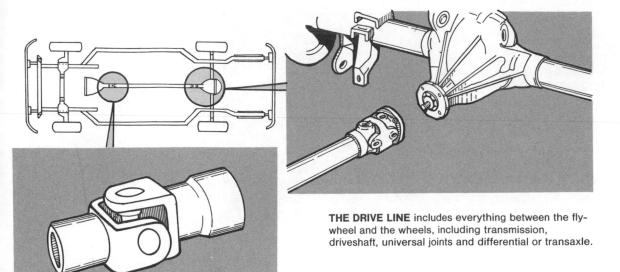

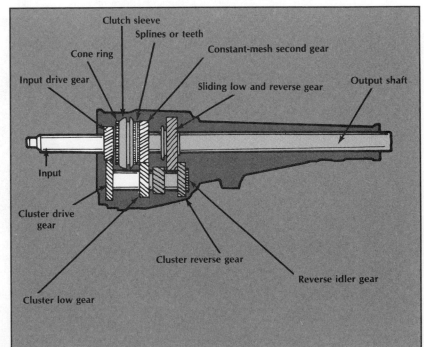

THE DRIVE LINE includes everything between the flywheel and the wheels, including transmission, driveshaft, universal joints and differential or transaxle.

transmission is a box with clutches, bands, planetary gears and a torque converter. In the torque converter, the impeller, attached to the flywheel, forces transmission fluid against the vanes of a turbine, causing it to rotate. The turbine is attached to the transmission shaft providing power output to the wheels.

The *differential* assembly, also called the *rear end* in rear-drive cars, transfers the power from the driveshaft to the two drive wheels. It lets the outside wheel turn faster than the inside wheel when the car is making a turn (the outside wheel

has a greater distance to travel in the same time and must turn faster). Without this device, the drive wheels would skid or slide around turns, causing tire damage and handling problems.

Drive line service

Most of the parts of the drive line involve the kind of equipment and skills that are often best left to the professional technician. Automatic transmission fluid and filter service, however, is one aspect of car repair that is frequently ignored. Auto maker suggestions regarding this

IN A CAR with manual transmission, the gears in the drive train are selected by a hand-operated gearshift and foot-operated clutch.

Clutch sleeve
Splines or teeth
Cone ring
Constant-mesh second gear
Input drive gear
Sliding low and reverse gear
Output shaft
Input
Cluster drive gear
Cluster reverse gear
Reverse idler gear
Cluster low gear

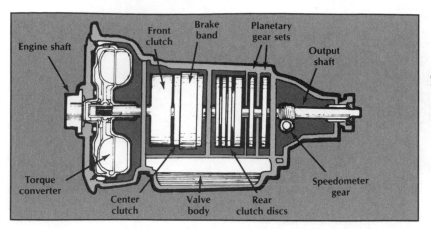

CARS WITH AUTOMATIC TRANSMISSION select gear ratios automatically by a system of bands and plates moved by special transmission fluid.

type of service vary widely. Some recommend no change until 100,000 miles for normal service, yet suggest a change at 15,000 miles for vehicles that tow trailers. If you plan to keep your car for more than a year or two, regularly scheduled transmission service is a good idea. An interval of 25,000 miles is probably just about right for vehicles used in mixed city and highway driving with varying loads, while 15,000 is about right for vehicles frequently overloaded, used continually in heavy city traffic or used to tow trailers.

To service the unit, warm the car to operating temperature by driving it. Raise the car on four jackstands that are securely positioned. With a catch pan standing ready, remove the drain plug (if there is one) from the transmission's oil pan. If it doesn't have a drain plug, begin removing the transmission pan bolts. Leave two or three bolts in one corner of the pan and, with the drain pan under the opposite corner of the transmission sump, begin loosening them. Pry the pan loose and let the fluid pour out of one corner of the oil pan into the drain pan. Continue to loosen the remaining bolts as the flow subsides, carefully removing them completely once the flow stops. There will still be quite a bit of fluid in the pan. Pour it carefully into the drain pan.

After the oil pan has been removed, clean it thoroughly. Check the pan. A certain amount of clutch dust is normal, and even a small quantity of powdered metal might be normal in some transmissions, but if there are larger chips or pieces of metal, suspect serious trouble. Inspect the fluid you have drained. Some darkening is

Automatic transmission (oil pan removed)

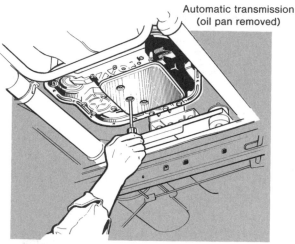

TRANSMISSION OIL filter can be changed once the oil pan has been removed. Note the condition of the oil and the correct placement of any gaskets and O-rings.

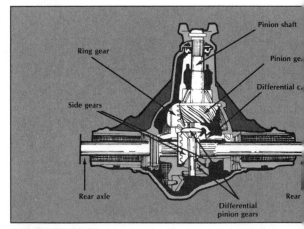

THE DIFFERENTIAL allows one wheel to turn at a different speed from the other while it transmits power from the driveshaft to the axles. This is also called the "rear end" on rear-drive cars. On front-drive cars, the differential and transmission are combined in a single unit called the *transaxle*.

okay, but a burnt or rotten egg smell and brown or black discoloration are signs of internal problems.

Remove the filter from the bottom of the transmission. It's held in place by one or more bolts or by clips. Replace the filter with the correct unit. Don't forget to reinstall any gaskets or O-rings you find between the filter and the transmission.

Clean the pan with solvent and a brush, and scrape the gasket off. Clean the transmission's mating surface before reinstalling the pan and gasket. Start all of the pan bolts with your fingers before reinstalling the pan. Then, in a crisscross pattern, torque them to about 10 ft.-lb. with a torque wrench.

Refill the transmission through the dipstick tube with the type of ATF fluid specified by the car maker. Use only the fluid specified in your owner's manual. Once you think you've added enough, start the engine, let it run for a while, shift the transmission through gears and return the selector to **PARK**. With the vehicle idling in **PARK** check the fluid level and add more if necessary. Check under the car for any fluid leaks.

Procedures to service drive line parts

Do-it-yourself procedures for servicing your car's **Transmission and Drive Line** are in Volume 25. There you'll find diagnostic procedures for troubleshooting power train noise. You'll also find directions on how to avoid automatic transmission problems and adjust the cable-operated shift mechanism on front-drive cars, and a troubleshooting guide for differentials.

STEERING AND SUSPENSION SYSTEMS

How your car's steering and suspension systems work

The suspension system permits the front and rear wheels to move up and down independently so your car remains level and steady. The suspension system gives your car roadability.

The *frame* supports the weight of the engine, transmission, body and passengers. It is in turn supported by the *springs,* which keep the car level if a wheel hits a bump or pothole. As the bump forces the wheel upward, the spring begins to compress. The *shock absorber,* mounted between the frame and the control arm, slows down the compression action of the spring. When the wheel clears the bump, the spring expands. The shock absorber slows down the expanding action of the spring. The spring action is reversed when the wheel rolls into a pothole.

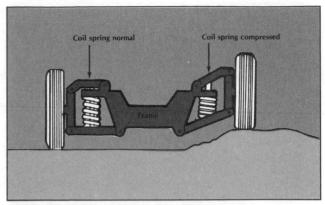

SPRINGS SUPPORT THE car's frame and keep the front of the car level if a front wheel hits a bump or pothole.

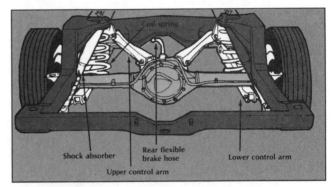

ON CARS WITH rear coil springs, control arms and track rods allow the rear wheels to move up and down while keeping them in line with the frame.

In the *MacPherson strut* independent suspension, the coil spring and shock absorber are one combined unit. The entire strut assembly is attached to the unitized frame by a rubber-insulated top mount. The lower end of the assembly is attached to the wheel spindle. The lower control arm is attached to the underbody and to the spindle.

Maintaining the steering and suspension system parts

Proper lubrication, done when you give your car a lube job, is about all you would want to do with most of the steering and suspension system parts. Shock absorbers, however, can be easily tested—without any tools—and replaced. Standing at any corner of the car, place your hands on the bumper or fender and press down with as much force as you can. When the corner reaches its maximum downward point, let up. Keep

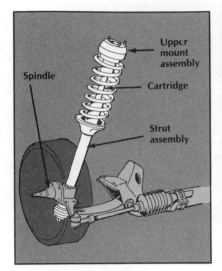

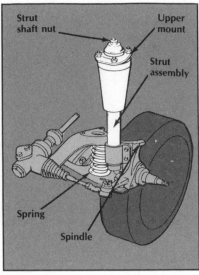

IN THE MACPHERSON strut, the shock absorber is built into the strut housing and the coil spring and shock absorber are one combined unit.

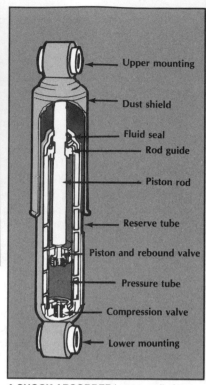

A SHOCK ABSORBER has two cylinders; the upper slips over the lower, allowing the shock to control movement as it moves either up or down.

doing this until the car is rocking up and down. While the car is rocking on a downward stroke, when the corner has been pushed down to its maximum point, quickly remove your hands. If the body comes up one time and settles level, the shock absorber in that corner is probably okay. If the body bounces up and down again instead of settling level in a smooth manner, the shock absorber in that corner is weak and probably should be replaced. Do this test at each corner of the car. For even suspension action, always replace shocks in pairs—both front shocks or both rears. *Never replace only one shock.*

The strut assembly of a MacPherson strut should be checked closely for spring fatigue, poor damping characteristics, binding and popping when the wheels are turned. Check also for leaks between the shock shaft and strut housing. By bouncing the suspension, check for binding. This could indicate a bent strut. If any of these conditions exist, the strut will have to be taken apart for service or replaced. This is a job for a professional. Again, always rebuild or replace struts in pairs, not singly.

Procedures to check and service steering and suspension system parts

Our do-it-yourself guide for the **Suspension and Steering System** is in Volume 23. There you'll find tips on keeping the parts of the systems working, followed by specific help for understanding, maintaining, and replacing your shock absorbers.

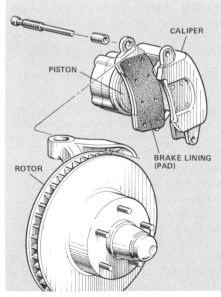

IN DISC BRAKES, the fluid in the caliper moves the pistons, which forces the friction pads against the disc, stopping the car.

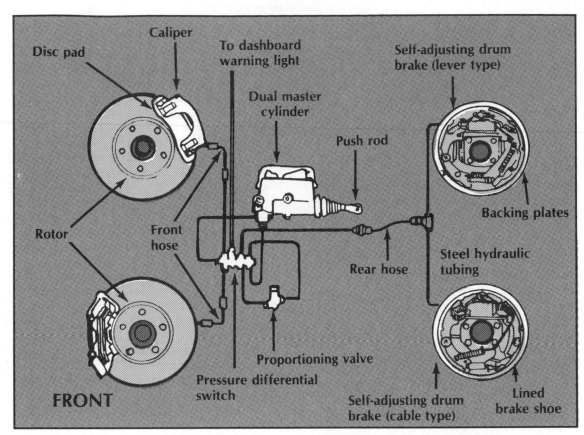

Disc pad — **Caliper** — **To dashboard warning light** — **Self-adjusting drum brake (lever type)** — **Dual master cylinder** — **Push rod** — **Rotor** — **Front hose** — **Backing plates** — **Rear hose** — **Steel hydraulic tubing** — **Proportioning valve** — **Pressure differential switch** — **FRONT** — **Self-adjusting drum brake (cable type)** — **Lined brake shoe**

WHEN YOU PUSH on the brake pedal, the master cylinder piston forces brake fluid through steel lines and brake hoses to each of the wheel cylinders or calipers. The calipers or wheel-cylinder pistons push the pads or brake shoes against the rotors or brake drums. The friction developed by the pads against the rotors or drums stops a wheel from turning.

BRAKES

How your brakes work

Cars today have a four-wheel hydraulic braking system to retard all four wheels, allowing the car to stop in a straight line.

In the past, a four-wheel drum-brake-shoe system was adequate, but it had one major drawback. Because of the excessive heat buildup, the brakes faded or lost their power to stop the car. To overcome this problem, disc brakes were introduced. The disc brake is superior because it deals with heat more effectively.

When you step on the brakes, momentum throws most of the car's weight forward. Over 60 percent of the braking force is exerted by the front wheels. For balanced braking it is necessary to have more braking capacity there, so the front brakes are usually the disc-type, with drum-type on the rear wheels.

Drum brakes. The drum-brake system, with Bendix servo and self-energizing action, minimizes the amount of pedal pressure necessary to stop the car. This is done by hooking a spring and adjusting screw from the heel of the primary brake shoe (the lower end of the forward shoe) to the toe of the secondary brake shoe (the lower end of the back shoe). Since this system uses one spring to anchor both shoes at one end, it allows the other end of both shoes to move freely and simultaneously. When pressure is put on the foot pedal, fluid in the master cylinder, hydraulic lines and wheel cylinders moves the pistons in the wheel cylinders outward. The pistons force the top ends of the brake shoes out against the drum. The forward (primary) shoe tends to lock to the revolving brake drum and tries to turn with it. As the forward shoe tries to turn with the drum, it pushes the back (secondary) shoe against the drum. The secondary shoe tries to turn with the drum, but it is anchored at the top so it jams into the drum, locks it and stops the wheel from turning.

Disc brakes. The disc-brake system uses a

heavy disc in place of a drum and brake-friction pads in place of brake shoes and linings. In place of the wheel cylinder, a caliper is bolted to the wheel spindle so the friction pads on the caliper can sandwich the disc between them. When you put pressure on the brake pedal, the fluid in the caliper moves the pistons, forcing the friction pads against the disc, stopping the car.

Brake system service

The drum brakes on most cars today have automatic brake adjusters to maintain proper pedal height as the brakes wear. On most cars, the adjusters are activated when you put on the brakes while the car is moving backward. If you have to push your brake pedal down more than a couple of inches before the brakes begin to take hold, find a safe area away from traffic and apply the brakes firmly several times while moving in reverse. If this fails to bring the pedal up to an acceptable height, remove the brake drums and inspect the adjusters to see if they are jammed or rusted.

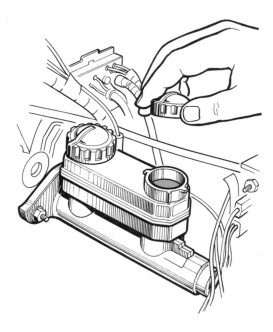

FLUID LEVEL IN the master cylinder should be within ¼ to ½ inch of the top lip. Some fluid level drop is normal on cars with disc brakes as pads wear.

Disc brakes are designed so they don't require periodic adjustment. As the linings slowly wear out and the brake pedal is applied, the piston in the caliper slowly moves out toward the rotor to compensate for brake pad wear. The area displaced directly behind the piston is slowly filled with brake fluid. For this reason, disc brakes require more brake fluid in the system.

You should adjust the parking brake when you have to move the foot pedal or handle a greater distance than usual to apply the brake (usually more than five to seven clicks).

Inspect the linings at least once a year—more often if you do a lot of driving or drive constantly in heavy stop-and-go city traffic. If they are allowed to wear excessively, the metal rivets holding the linings to the shoe, or the steel back of the brake shoe itself, may grind grooves in the drum's braking surface. When this happens, the drum will have to be resurfaced (ground down) or replaced if it is beyond specified tolerances.

Remove one of the front wheels and inspect the brake disc, caliper and linings. There is an inspection hole in most calipers so you can see the linings; don't get any oil or grease on them. If the pads are worn to within .030 inch of the surface of the steel shoe, replace both sets of shoe and lining-pad assemblies.

If the caliper is cracked or there is evidence of fluid leaking through the casting, it must be replaced as a unit. While you have the wheel off to inspect the linings and pads, inspect the hydraulic brake lines. Look for cracks, leaks, lines that have become thin by rubbing against a suspension part, and any other signs of wear or deterioration.

Check the level of brake fluid in the master cylinder every time you change engine oil. Checking the level is easy. Clean off the cylinder cover, remove the cap and look at the fluid level. If it is low (more than ¼ to ½ inch below the "Full" mark or the top edge of the reservoir), add only the approved-type heavy-duty brake fluid specified in your owner's manual. On cars with disc brakes, it's normal for the fluid level to drop as the brake pads wear. Fluid level should never be allowed to reach the bottom of the reservoir, or air will enter the system.

Procedures for brake system maintenance

Our do-it-yourself procedures for **Brake System** maintenance are in Volume 4. There you'll find a troubleshooting guide for brakes, followed by how-to-do-it procedures for an overhaul of a drum brake system and how to replace disc brake pads.

Bandsaw basics

■ IF FOR SOME reason stationary tools had to be stripped from your shop, but you could choose just one to keep, it would probably be the bandsaw. A bandsaw is a relatively simple machine consisting of a pair of wheels around which a blade travels, a table for supporting the workpiece, and guides for keeping the blade running and cutting in accurate fashion. A well-maintained bandsaw is one of the most valuable tools you can add to your workshop. With it, you can make simple rips and crosscuts; the better-quality tools also are equipped with adjustable tables for making compound cuts.

If you own a model with a fair-sized throat—that's the distance from the blade to the vertical blade enclosure—you can handle most of the ripping and crosscutting chores that you're likely

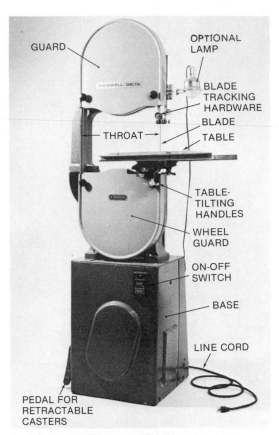

BANDSAW PARTS are identified on this 14-in. saw. Capacity is blade-arm distance, or throat.

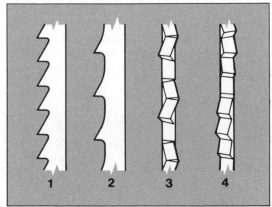

BANDSAW BLADES you should know: 1 Regular teeth for ferrous metals and wood. 2 Skip tooth has wide-spaced teeth for high-speed cutting, fast chip clearance. 3 Wavy-set hacksaw-like blade for tubing and pipe. 4 Raker set, a general purpose blade usually used on thick stock for a fast cut.

to encounter. And the bandsaw gives you super-capacity for cutting scrolls, curves and the like, which are impossible on the table, or radial-arm saw.

Like the table saw, the bandsaw is a bench tool. It should be well fastened to a rigid base—either legs designed for it, or a bench that puts the saw's table at a comfortable height. Position the saw in your shop so that there is room in all directions for swinging a workpiece. Fit bandsaw legs with lockable casters. When the tool is not in use, it can be parked along a wall. When you need plenty of working room, simply push the table to shop center and lock the casters.

If you are buying a bandsaw, do read the manufacturer's instructions for using and maintaining the tool.

Be aware that there is a wide variety of blades available. Since they vary in tooth size and configuration, you should know which types are best for your purposes; there really isn't one general-purpose blade. Make no mistake, you need a number of different blades in order to get the maximum performance from your bandsaw.

The blades come in widths ranging from ⅛ to

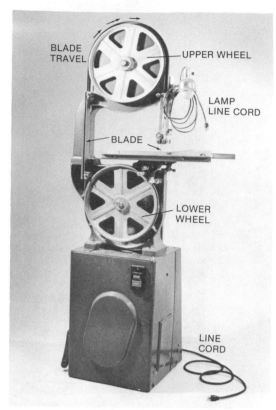

WITH WHEEL GUARDS (covers) removed, it is easy to understand principle of bandsaw cutting. Under tension, blade travels around both wheels.

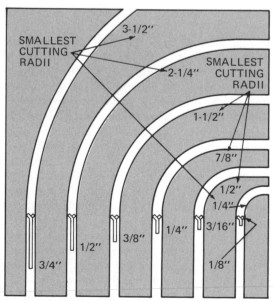

BLADES ARE available in widths from ⅛ to ¾ in. Narrower ones can make the tightest turns; wide ones are useful for heavy stock.

TABLE INSERT should always be in place when the saw is in use to support the workpiece. It is removed to get the blade in and out (using the table slot visible in the foreground).

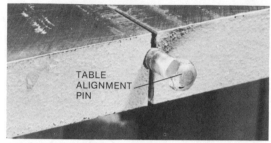

TABLE-ALIGNMENT pin keeps the saw table level on both sides of the blade-changing slot.

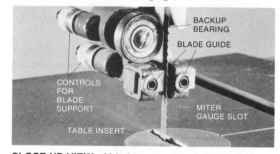

CLOSE-UP VIEW of blade support and guides reveals the basic simplicity of design. Blade guides should ride just behind the gullets while the backup bearing supports the blade as the work is fed into the teeth. Entire assembly can be adjusted up or down to suit depth of cut required.

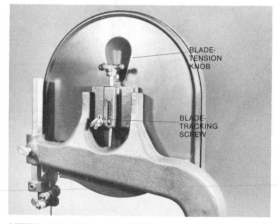

AFTER A BLADE is installed it must be tensioned and tracked using this hardware.

MAKE CERTAIN thumbs are not in the cutting line as you push workpiece into the blade.

TO COMPLETE a rip on narrow stock, push work through with a wide board (arrow).

GRIP WORK and gauge firmly with your fingers when making crosscuts with the miter gauge.

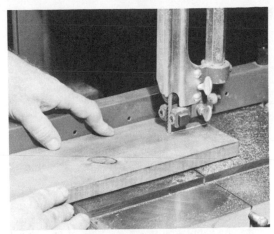

WHEN ACCURACY is a must on a long rip, use rip fence and position hands as shown.

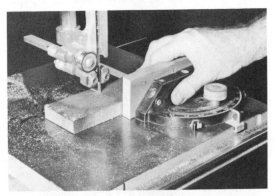

A MITER GAUGE comes with a quality saw; add an extension block of wood for greater support.

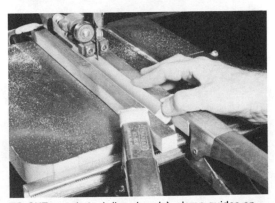

TO CUT round stock (i.e. dowels), clamp guides on both sides so the work can't drift.

¾-in. The narrow ones can cut to a tighter radius than the wide ones. If you try to turn too sharp a radius with a wide blade, you're sure to break it.

It is best to use the small-tooth blades when you want a fairly smooth cut that won't require a great deal of sanding. These cut slower than the large-tooth blades, which leave saw marks that have to be removed with sandpaper. When making cuts where roughness doesn't matter at all, use a skip-tooth blade, which permits extra-fast cutting.

To use the bandsaw, position yourself comfortably in front of the table and feed the work slowly. The workpiece should not be shoved forcefully against the blade and, if the blade binds, back the work off to remove pressure until the blade again runs smoothly.

Keep your saw adjusted to the maker's instructions. Correct tension is necessary for proper tracking. When possible, use one of the cutting guides as shown in the photo.

Bandsaw tips from the experts

■ STILL THE BEST and only tool for making curved cuts in thick stock, a bandsaw far outperforms the sabre saw in smoothness of cut, speed and tight turns. There's a trick to making tight turns even when using a narrow blade, and especially when the work calls for turns as small as ½-in. radius. A series of straight cuts is first made in from the edge of the work to the line of cut, dividing up the curve in segments as shown. As you follow the curve with the saw, the waste falls free, giving the blade more room to make the turn. This stunt not only permits tight turns, but it keeps the blade from heating and burning the wood in negotiating turns of short radii.

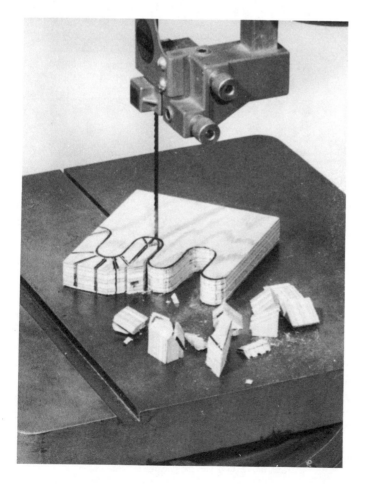

A WOODEN V-BLOCK cut on your circular saw to cradle the work makes your bandsaw extra handy for kerfing the end of turning squares, as well as for splitting dowels and doing other cylindrical work down the middle. In each case, the block is clamped in position to the bandsaw table so that the V-cut bisects the blade precisely.

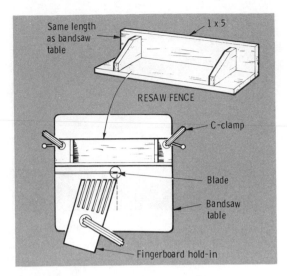

EDGE-RIPPING wide stock into thin boards is a job only a bandsaw can handle. It requires the use of a wooden fence to support and guide the work on edge, plus a slotted fingerboard to hold the work firmly against the fence. A ⅜ or ½-in.-wide skip-tooth blade is best, and a push stick is a must in feeding the work safely past the blade. Note the position of the hold-in board in relation to the blade. A series of parallel saw kerfs gives a spring action to the fingerboard when it presses against the work.

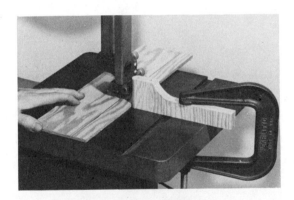

WHEN YOU FIND that the blade has a tendency to drift away from the cutting line while doing repeat ripping, a pivot fence clamped to the saw table will solve the problem. Having a rounded nose, the center of which is positioned to align with the front edge of the blade, the fence allows the work to be maneuvered to compensate for drift as the work is passed through the blade. The fence, of course, is located a distance from the blade equal to the width of the finished work. The work is held against the pivot fence at all times.

MASS RIPPING of identical widths on a bandsaw means less kerf waste than that created by a bench saw; this can add up to a considerable saving when cutting pieces in large quantities. If your saw is not already equipped with a fence, you can improvise one by clamping a wood strip to the table, using a try square to align it with the front of the table and parallel with the blade. A wide blade works best in straight ripping operations since it will not tend to drift as much as a narrow blade. It will always pay to switch to a wider blade.

WHEN IT COMES to cutting perfect discs of any size, you can't beat a bandsaw and a circle-cutting jig. With the work impaled on an adjustable pivot point, you cut a perfect circle by merely rotating the work. The drawing below shows how the jig is made, designed to clamp to the edge of the bandsaw table. The size of the stock must be roughly the diameter of the disc to be cut so that the blade is on line when it enters the wood.

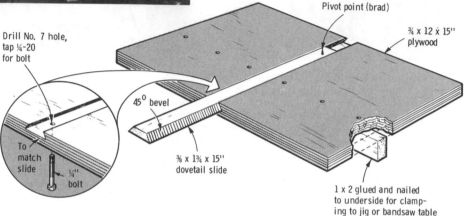

Drill No. 7 hole, tap ¼-20 for bolt

To match slide

¼" bolt

45° bevel

⅜ x 1¾ x 15" dovetail slide

Pivot point (brad)

¾ x 12 x 15" plywood

1 x 2 glued and nailed to underside for clamping to jig or bandsaw table

WITH ITS TABLE tilted 45° and a wooden fence clamped to it, your bandsaw provides a quick way of roughing turning squares "in the round" prior to working the piece on a lathe. The fence is positioned so that corners of the work are ripped off.

TO AVOID BECOMING "pocketed" when cutting a scroll in which two curves meet, always saw in first from the edge to the point of the pocket. The kerf frees waste when you reach the pocket, eliminating backtracking. Complete the cut from the opposite end.

Rip fence for your bandsaw

HOLE TO SUIT 10d NAIL

ACTUAL-SIZE CAM LEVER

3/4 x 3-1/2 x 5"

THREE 3/4" PIECES

GRIPPER

SCREW EYE

SPRING

CAM LEVER

10d NAILS, PRESS FIT

3/4 x 1-1/4 x 4"

LOCKED POSITION

5-1/2"

UNLOCKED POSITION

WOOD TABLE

■ A RIP FENCE on a bandsaw can be as handy as the one on a table saw, yet how many bandsaws come with a fence as standard equipment? You can make this wooden one for your bandsaw; it works as well as any fence you can buy—and costs a lot less. Its cam-locking action is positive and holds the fence securely to front and back edges of the table. When the clamping lever is released, the fence stays put, yet can be moved back and forth or lifted from the table.

The drawing shows how the fence is made, its length being determined by the depth of the bandsaw table. The coil spring, housed in a 2¼-in.-long notch which is made in the center member of the three-piece fence, keeps the fence snug against the saw table when you make lateral adjustment. Overall length of the center piece should be ⅛-in. less than table depth.

While the cutaway drawing that illustrates the fence in an unlocked position shows the spring-fitted pressure pad backed off from the table, this is shown exaggerated for the sake of clarity. Actually, the spring causes the pressure pad to hug the table even when unlocked.

Drop-on table for your bandsaw

■ **THERE ARE TIMES** when even the largest bandsaw table is too small for the job. By adding this auxiliary wood table, you can increase a small table to a king-size 20 x 37-incher with a rip fence and circle-cutting attachment.

This table is unique in that the rip fence and pivot point stay put in any set position by mere friction. To shift position of either fence or disc pivot, just pick it up and place it where you want it.

Three cleats, attached underneath, position and hold the plywood over the table. Rip fence and pivot point ride in a ¾-in.-wide dado having a strip of No. 120 emery cloth glued to the bot-

tom. Make the dado with your router or saw's dado cutter, and cut the ¾-in.-wide blade slot with parallel cuts on your table saw. Depth of the dado should equal the combined thickness of metal, rubber and emery cloth.

The two metal hooks rest in ⅛-in.-deep dadoes and are bent. Make the short bends first, hook them over the edge and mark for the second bend. Bend by heating the metal with a propane torch before clamping and bending in your vise.

Bike inner tubes are better than car inner tubes to cover the metal pieces. Clean and cement with super glue. Pivot pin in a No. 6 x ½-in. fh stovebolt filed to a point.

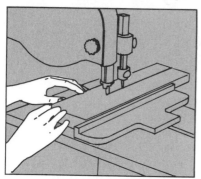

TABLE CAN BE made to fit any size saw. Here it's on a 14-in. Rockwell with its rip fence in use. Photo below shows how pivot point is used to saw a perfect disc. Cleat spacing at right is for 12-in. Craftsman. Cleats are placed to suit saw's table.

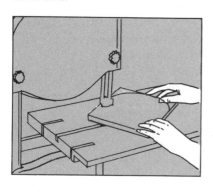

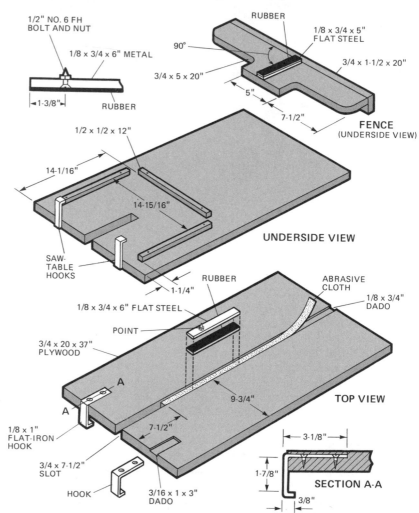

1/2" NO. 6 FH BOLT AND NUT
1/8 x 3/4 x 6" METAL
1-3/8"
RUBBER

RUBBER
1/8 x 3/4 x 5" FLAT STEEL
90°
3/4 x 5 x 20"
5"
3/4 x 1-1/2 x 20"
7-1/2"
FENCE (UNDERSIDE VIEW)

1/2 x 1/2 x 12"
14-1/16"
14-15/16"
UNDERSIDE VIEW
SAW-TABLE HOOKS
1-1/4"

RUBBER
ABRASIVE CLOTH
1/8 x 3/4 x 6" FLAT STEEL
1/8 x 3/4 DADO
POINT
3/4 x 20 x 37" PLYWOOD
9-3/4"
TOP VIEW
A
A
1/8 x 1" FLAT-IRON HOOK
7-1/2"
3/4 x 7-1/2" SLOT
HOOK
3/16 x 1 x 3" DADO
3-1/8"
1-7/8"
SECTION A-A
3/8"

Redwood barbecue cart

■ THIS BARBECUE CART is designed to withstand exposure to heat and moisture and to fulfill specific outdoor living needs. To begin with, kiln-dried, clear, heartwood redwood was used throughout. This grade is very smooth and free of blemishes and warps. It's also lightweight, structurally stable and highly water-resistant.

Subassemblies and materials

The unit is constructed of two separate assemblies: a case that contains the drawers, storage bin, cutting board and broiler pan; and a framework that acts as the basic structural support for the case and for the top and shelf boards. When reviewing the materials list for this project, keep in mind that architectural-grade 2 x 4s were used for the legs. These measure 1⅝ x 3½ in. If you use construction-grade stock instead, adjust the materials list to reflect the narrower 1½-in. thickness.

Assembly is made with waterproof resorcinol glue and finished with three coats of satin finish to help withstand the elements.

Construction details

Begin building the framework by cutting the legs and rails to size. Then cut the dadoes in the legs as shown in the drawing to receive the lower shelf rails. The end rails are let completely into the legs and the side rails are joined with half-lap joints. Also, cut to size the add-on wheel blocks that form the support for the wheel axles. Join these blocks to the inside of the wheel legs with glue and four 4d finishing nails per joint. Clamp and let dry.

Then, using a router with a ⅜-in.-rad. rounding-over bit, ease the upper half of each leg edge as shown in the photo. Stop approximately 3¼ in. below the leg top. This will leave the leg top square for maximum gluing surface later when the rails and cases are attached to the legs. Also, by starting the cuts halfway up the legs, the lower half of each remains square for joining the lower rails. Later, when the rails are glued in place, fin-

ish the round job by moving the router down the legs and across the rails in one continuous cut.

Bore the wheel axle holes in the wheel legs. Fabricate the wheels by gluing together two squares of 1 x 6 stock with the grain direction of each running at right angles to the other. Clamp until dry, then lay out a 4½-in.-dia. circle on each block. Bore a 1-in.-dia. blade entry hole on the waste side of the circumference line, then cut out the wheel using a sabre saw with a pivot guide as shown. Sand the wheels smooth and bore an axle hole through the center of each. Cut the aluminum rod for the axles, and test-fit both.

Next, glue and clamp the lower side rails to the legs. Let dry, then join the lower end rails to the legs using glue and screws. Cut the sliding shelf notch in one end rail, then clamp all upper rails onto the legs. Bore screw plug and shank holes into the rails and pilot holes into the legs. Separate, apply glue and attach the rails with screws.

Attach the shelf slat support cleats to the lower rails with glue and clamps. Then glue and clamp the cleats and the spacers to the upper rails.

Case assembly

Cut the case sides and ends to size. Cut out the drawer, door and bin pockets in the case sides using a table saw and radial-arm saw. You can also use a sabre saw to make these cuts. Just clamp a guide fence in the proper position for each cut so they will be straight and square. Also, bore a small hole in the corner of each opening—on the waste side of the lines—for blade entry.

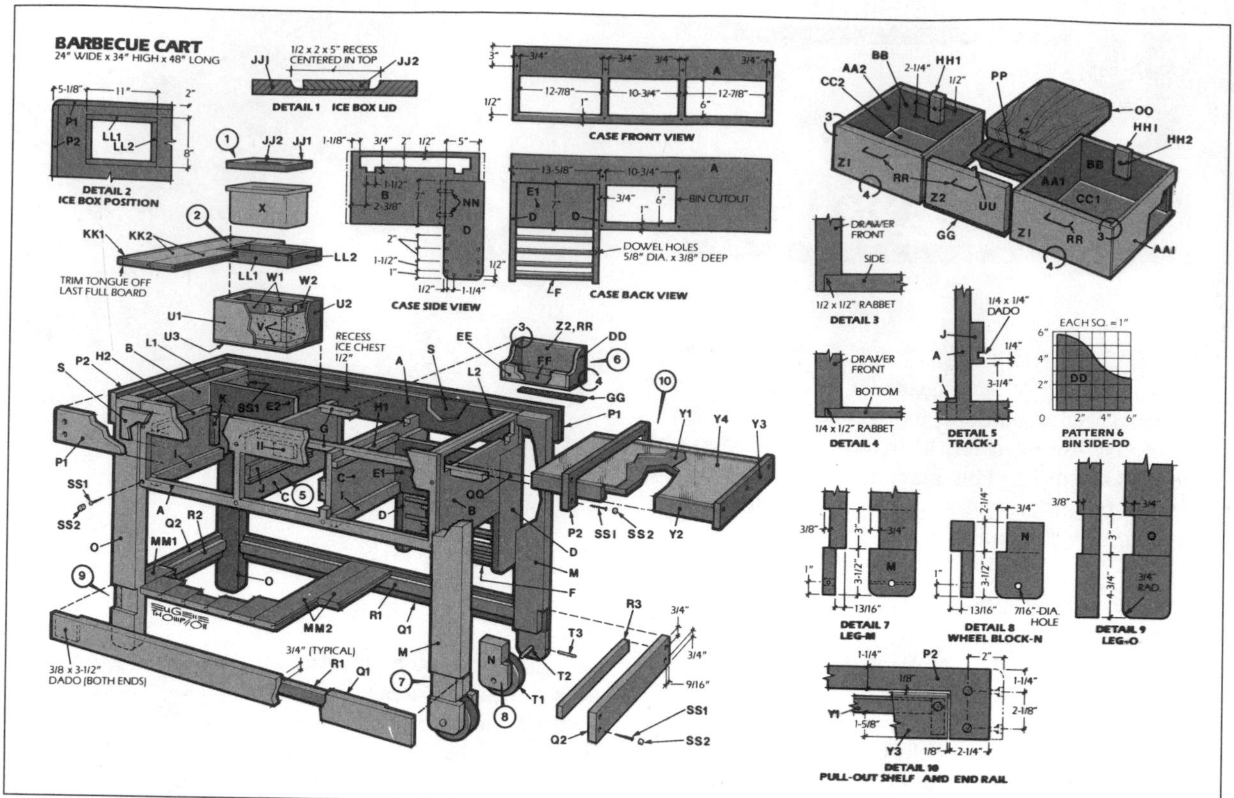

MATERIALS LIST
BARBECUE CART

Key	No.	Size and description (use)
A	2	¾ x 11¼ x 39½" redwood (case side)
B	2	¾ x 11¼ x 20¼" redwood (case end)
C	2	¾ x 8¾ x 20¼" redwood (case partition)
D	2	¾ x 5¾ x 15" redwood (bottle rack side)
E1	1	¾ x 7 x 12⅞" redwood (bottle rack partition)
E2	1	¾ x 4 x 12⅞" redwood (ice-box partition)
F	9	⅝"-dia. x 12⅞" hardwood dowel
G	2	¾ x 1½ x 29⅝" redwood (side track)
H1	2	¾ x ¾ x 14½" redwood (upper drawer guide)
H2	2	¾ x ¾ x 11½" redwood (upper drawer guide)
I	4	¾ x 1⅛ x 14½" redwood (lower drawer guide)
J	2	¾ x 1½ x 14½" redwood (board, pan track)
K	2	¾ x ¾ x 5" redwood (drawer stop block)
L1	1	¾ x 2 x 19¼" redwood (top cleat)
L2	1	⅜ x ¾ x 19¼" redwood (top cleat)
M	2	1⅝ x 3½ x 32" redwood (wheel leg)
N	2	1⅝ x 3½ x 5¾" redwood (wheel block)
O	2	1⅝ x 3½ x 33¼" redwood (straight leg)
P1	2	¾ x 4 x 48" redwood (top side rail)
P2	2	¾ x 4 x 22½" redwood (top end rail)
Q1	2	¾ x 3 x 46½" redwood (shelf side rail)
Q2	2	¾ x 3 x 21¾" redwood (shelf end rail)
R1	2	¾ x 1¼ x 39½" redwood (shelf cleat)
R2	1	¾ x 1¼ x 19¼" redwood (shelf cleat)
R3	1	¾ x 1¼ x 16" redwood (shelf cleat)
S	2	⅜ x 3 x 39½" plywood (spacer)
T1	2	1½" x 4½"-dia. redwood (wheel)
T2	2	7/16"-dia. x 3½" aluminum rod (axle)
T3	2	3/32"-dia. x 2¼" brass rod (axle pin)
U1	2	¼ x 5⅞ x 11" plywood (ice-box front, back)
U2	2	¼ x 5⅞ x 7½" plywood (ice-box end)
U3	1	¼ x 8 x 11" plywood (ice-box bottom)
V	2 sq. ft.	¾"-thick Styrofoam insulation, cut to fit
W1	2	¾ x 1¼ x 10½" redwood (block)
W2	2	¾ x 1¼ x 6" redwood (block)
X	1	Freezette No. 336, 4½-qt. plastic bowl (ice bowl)
Y1	1	¾ x 16 x 29¼" plywood (shelf)
Y2	2	¾ x 1½ x 29¼" redwood (shelf side rail)
Y3	1	¾ x 2⅝ x 17¾" redwood (shelf end rail)
Y4	1	1/16 x 16 x 29¼" Wilsonart No. D30-6, Natural Almond plastic laminate
Z1	2	¾ x 5¾ x 12¾" redwood (drawer front)
Z2	2	¾ x 5¾ x 10⅝" redwood (door, bin front)
AA1	2	½ x 5½ x 15" plywood (drawer side)
AA2	2	½ x 5½ x 12" plywood (drawer side)
BB	2	½ x 5½ x 11¾" plywood (drawer back)
CC1	1	¼ x 12¾ x 15" plywood (drawer bottom)
CC2	1	¼ x 12¾ x 12" plywood (drawer bottom)
DD	2	½ x 5⅝ x 5¾" plywood (bin side)
EE	1	½ x 2¼ x 9⅝" plywood (bin back)
FF	1	¼ x 5¾ x 10⅝" plywood (bin bottom)
GG	2	1½ x 10½" aluminum continuous hinge
HH1	2	½ x 1½ x 3½" redwood (drawer stop)
HH2	2	¾" No. 8 flathead screw
II	1	¾ x 1½ x 3" redwood (door catch block)
JJ1	1	¾ x 6½ x 9½" redwood (ice-box top)
JJ2	1	½ x ¾ x 3¾" redwood (ice-box handle)
KK1	2	½ x ¾ x 22½" redwood (top end slat)
KK2	14	¾ x 3¼ x 22½" redwood (top slat)
LL1	2	¾ x 1¼ x 11" redwood (ice-box frame)
LL2	2	¾ x 1¼ x 6½" redwood (ice-box frame)
MM1	2	¾ x 3 x 21" redwood (shelf end slat)
MM2	13	¾ x 3¼ x 21" redwood (shelf slat)
NN	2	⅜"-dia. x 2" hardwood dowel
OO	1	13/16 x 10½ x 14½" maple (cutting board)
PP	1	broiler pan
QQ	2	24" full-extension drawer slide
RR	4	3" aluminum pull with aluminum bases
SS1	51	1½" No. 8 flathead screw
SS2	43	½"-dia. x ¼" redwood plug
UU	1	cabinet catch

ONE SIDE OF THE CART has a center drop-down door (*left*) that covers a slide-out cutting board and broiler pan. A built-in bottle rack (*right*) provides storage for wine, spirits and mixes close to the ice chest.

USE A DADO HEAD in a radial-arm saw to cut shelf rail dadoes in legs. By installing a higher fence in the table, the cut through it serves as a leg cut alignment guide.

THE CUT LEG PARTS are ready for assembly. The two center legs, and blocks between, form the axle support for wheels. The others are single legs for cart front.

JOIN THE WHEEL BLOCKS to the rear legs using glue and four 4d finishing nails per joint. Set nailheads and let the assembly dry overnight before continuing.

SLIDE EACH RAIL completely into its proper leg dado. Then use a utility knife to mark the precise width of the half-lap joint on the inside surface of the rail.

USE A ROUTER to round corners on the upper section of each leg before top rails are attached. Nail a block in place to stop the cutter 3¼ in. below the leg top.

GLUE UP 1 X 6 STOCK for the wheels, let dry, then draw a 4½-in.-dia. circle on the block. Bore blade entry hole on waste side of the line and cut using a sabre saw with pivot guide.

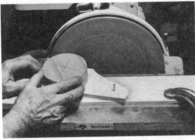

A SIMPLE DISC-SANDER JIG assures precise circular sanding. Place wheel onto projecting nail, then pivot jig until wheel touches disc. Rotate wheel until smooth.

GLUE AND CLAMP the long bottom rails to legs. Let dry, then clamp the other rails in place. Bore screw plug, shank and pilot holes through the rails and into the legs.

HERE IS THE COMPLETED FRAME. Support cleats for the top shelf boards are on the inside surface of the rails, and the cutout on the end rail is for the sliding shelf.

BEGIN CASE CONSTRUCTION by gluing up stock for the facing panels. Then, using a table saw, cut out drawer openings by holding board in place and raising handle.

MAKE VERTICAL DRAWER CUTS on a radial-arm saw. Use a square to align the blade center over opening center. Lock carriage in place, then lower blade into stock.

INSTALL BOTTLE RACK hanging dowels in case end, then join all parts with glue and screws. Test-fit extension slide tracks, then remove and finish-sand.

ATTACH CASE to frame by driving two screws through the inside of each case corner into the legs. Install slides, build shelf, then check shelf for proper fit.

INSTALL LOWER DRAWER GUIDES, then build drawers and check for fit. Install upper guides, cutting board and pan track, and the bin on the opposite cart side.

CUT TOP BOARDS to size, then install with glue and 1-in. brads driven through the tongue into the support cleats at a 45° angle. Keep V-joint side of boards down.

WHEN BOARDS REACH ICE-BOX PARTITION, install small frame boards as shown in drawing (*parts LL1 and LL2*). Cut remaining top boards to conform to opening.

CUT ICE-BOX TOP to size, then hold it in jig frame shown, made of 1¼-in.-wide stock. Install ¾-in. core box bit in router and cut depression using jig as fence.

Cut out the notch in the case side for the bottle rack and cut the bottle rack partition (part E1) to size. Then cut the opening for the sliding shelf in one case end as shown on the drawing. Also cut the bottle rack notch in the same board. Bore two ⅜-in.-dia. dowel holes—for supporting the bottle rack—in this notch, then glue the dowels in place.

Assemble the case ends and sides with glue and screws, check for square and let dry. Then cut the case partitions to size and install with glue and screws driven through the face of the case sides. Use two screws for each partition end. Install the bottle rack partition, between the case end and the first partition, with glue and 6d finishing nails.

Joining case to frame

Slide the case into the frame assembly and attach by driving two screws through the inside of each case corner into the corner of each abutting leg. Next, glue and clamp the lower drawer guides, cutting board and pan track in place.

Cut the parts for and assemble the drawers, bin and ice box. Test-fit each. Remove the drawers and install the upper guides. Attach the bin and drop-down door with continuous hinges, then glue and clamp the bottle rack in place.

Install the ice-box partition with glue and 6d finishing nails. Then hang the box from this partition and the top side rail with ¾-in. No. 8 flathead screws driven through the inside of the box into these supports. Cut and fit the rigid insulation to the interior of the box. Make the fit tight

so friction, instead of adhesive, holds the pieces in place.

Next, install the tracks for the pullout shelf extension slides. Then build the shelf and cover it with plastic laminate. Attach the slides to the bottom of the shelf and the top of the tracks with several mounting screws. Check for proper movement before installing the remaining screws.

Install the top and shelf boards with glue and 1-in. brads driven through the board tongues into the support cleats at a 45° angle. Set the heads. Be sure to install the boards with the V-joint face down so you end up with a smooth surface on the top.

Fill all screw holes with redwood plugs and all nail holes with redwood- or mahogany-colored wood filler. Then round over the outside corners of the top rails to a 1½-in. radius. Use a portable belt sander with an 80-grit abrasive belt to remove most of the stock, but stop short of the completed radius and finish the shaping by hand-sanding with 150-grit sandpaper.

Complete the router work by easing all exposed edges with a ⅜-in.-rad. rounding-over bit. Finish-sand the entire piece with 150-grit paper. Remove the dust and apply the finish.

Install the wheels, attach the pulls to the drawers, door and bin, and mount the magnetic catch for the door. Make the cutting board and finish with mineral oil. Then slide it and the broiler pan into their tracks. Finish up by boring a ½-in.-dia. hole in the bottom of the ice box to provide drainage, and by inserting the plastic bowl into the box.

Wrap a table around your barbecue

■ BY ADDING this redwood barbecue table to your back-yard cook center, barbecues are certain to be happier times for both guests and chef. It wraps around a standard-size 23-in.-dia. kettle-shape brazier that's 29-in. high.

You'll need about 98 ft. of 2 x 3-in. construction heart redwood. Other materials used are ⅜-in. exterior-grade plywood for gussets, epoxy or resorcinol waterproof glue, 3-in. hot-dipped galvanized finishing nails, 3-in. and 1¼-in. galvanized common nails and wax paper.

Begin by using a 30°/60° triangle to sketch the full-size pattern of half the frame section. Cut mitered ends for the six hub pieces using the jig shown and sabre saw. Use this jig to make left and righthand miters by turning the stock over as required. Also use it to make ¾-in. partial cuts parallel to the miter cut. Make the 1¼-in. middle cut freehand to cut off waste.

A fast-setting epoxy is good for joining the parts of the hexagonal hub. Just position two *alternate* pieces and tack-nail them onto the worktable. Insert wax paper under the joints, then apply epoxy and push the middle piece in place. Leave this first half of the hub tacked to the table to use as a guide for assembling the second half, but don't glue the halves together as yet. Position the halves together. Then place a scrap block in the center and locate the center mark of the hub by intersecting each joint with a straightedge.

Use a beam compass set at 12½ in. to draw the center circle. Cut along the curve with a sabre saw, then epoxy the two hub halves together.

Cut spoke pieces to length and use two 3-in. finishing nails to join each to the hub. Cut five rim sections with notched ends, bore small pilot holes and nail rims to the spokes.

A simple way to add the decking is by cutting only one set with both ends mitered and installing it on the rear center section. Use 3-in. common nails, two at each end, and bore pilot holes. Then cut one mitered end for the next six-piece

ADD-ON BARBECUE TABLE comes in handy for holding cooking gear and food ready to put on the fire. It also makes serving and cleanup easier.

section of decking and butt it against the first section. Nail it in place, leaving the free end overlapping the next spoke slightly. Repeat this for the remaining four pieces in that section. Tack-nail a straight strip of wood to serve as a guide and use a circular saw to cut off the waste ends.

Turn the table over and make the reinforcing gussets from ⅜-in. exterior plywood. Cut leg parts and assemble with glue and nails to form a T. Then glue and nail the top of the T to the table frame.

USE A JIG such as that shown below to cut mitered ends. Two 2 x 4s on edge make a good work surface. Set-tooth blade assures straight cuts.

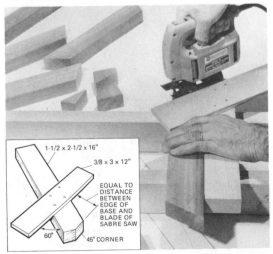

1-1/2 x 2-1/2 x 16"

3/8 x 3 x 12"

EQUAL TO DISTANCE BETWEEN EDGE OF BASE AND BLADE OF SABRE SAW

60°   45° CORNER

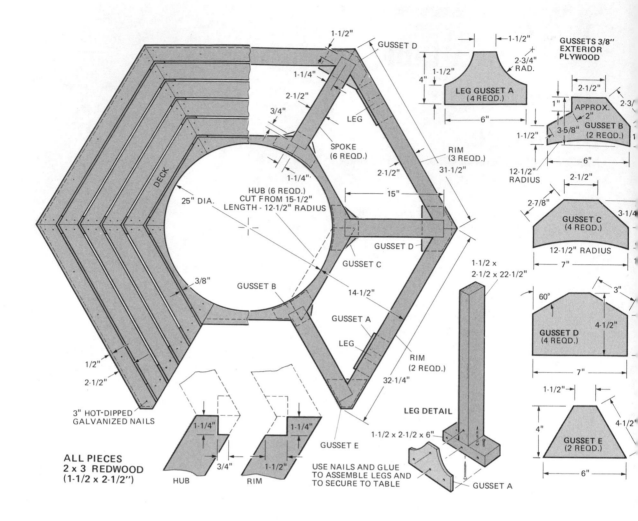

1-1/2"
GUSSET D
1-1/4"
2-1/2"
3/4"
LEG
SPOKE (6 REQD.)
1-1/4"
HUB (6 REQD.)
CUT FROM 15-1/2"
LENGTH - 12-1/2" RADIUS
25" DIA.
DECK
2-1/2"
15"
RIM (3 REQD.)
31-1/2"
GUSSET D
GUSSET C
14-1/2"
3/8"
GUSSET B
GUSSET A
LEG
RIM (2 REQD.)
32-1/4"
1/2"
2-1/2"
3" HOT-DIPPED GALVANIZED NAILS
ALL PIECES
2 x 3 REDWOOD
(1-1/2 x 2-1/2")

1-1/2"
1-1/2"
4"
2-3/4" RAD.
LEG GUSSET A (4 REQD.)
6"

GUSSETS 3/8"
EXTERIOR PLYWOOD

2-1/2"
1"
APPROX. 2"
2-3/
GUSSET B (2 REQD.)
3-5/8"
1-1/2"
12-1/2" RADIUS
6"

2-1/2"
2-7/8"
3-1/4
GUSSET C (4 REQD.)
12-1/2" RADIUS
7"

60°
3"
4-1/2"
GUSSET D (4 REQD.)
7"

1-1/2"
4"
4-1/2"
GUSSET E (2 REQD.)
6"

1-1/2 x 2-1/2 x 22-1/2"

LEG DETAIL

1-1/2 x 2-1/2 x 6"

GUSSET E

USE NAILS AND GLUE
TO ASSEMBLE LEGS AND
TO SECURE TO TABLE

GUSSET A

1-1/4"
3/4"
HUB

1-1/4"
1-1/2"
RIM

A BEAM COMPASS set at 12½ in. pivots at the center-marked block and marks a curve to be cut to accommodate the brazier.

CIRCULAR SAW shoe rides against a tacked-on guide strip to cut the diagonal joints. Set blade so that it won't cut the frame below.

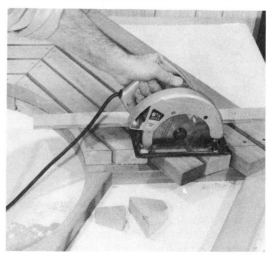

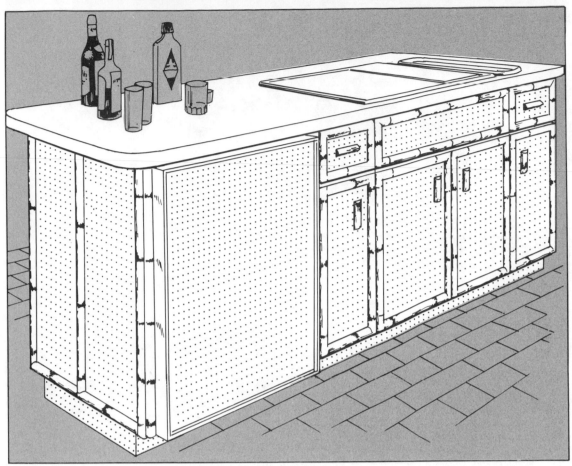

BARBECUE BAR with stove, refrigerator and food center is easy to build.

Barbecue bar for your family room

■ ALTHOUGH THIS BARBECUE bar is designed with special convenience features, it is easily constructed and finished with a durable plastic laminate. A twin-grill convertible cooktop, refrigerator and food center are incorporated into the bar. It is finished with butcher block and cane laminates and trimmed with rattan.

Materials left over from the bar will make a companion coffee table. A hinged top covers the table's storage area.

Cut bottom **I** and kickplate pieces **F, J.** Using glue and ringed nails join pieces, keeping assembly square.

Lay out and cut the two end panels **G** and at-tach to assembly with 8d finishing nails and white glue. Nail **Z** and **Y** to the refrigerator end panel, and nail a temporary 1 x 2 brace across the refrigerator opening.

Lay out and cut partitions **G** and **H.** Mark their locations on the plywood bottom. Turn the cabinet on its face (drawer) side, glue and nail partitions through the bottom with 8d nails.

Cut out the back **E.** With cabinet face down and everything square, nail and glue **E** in place. Nail rail **K** in partition notches.

Measure and cut facing pieces: horizontal rails **O, P, Q, R** and vertical stiles **S.** Use doweled joints on the facing frame. Dry assemble, then glue joints and clamp with 6-ft. bar clamps. Make sure assembly is square.

When facing frame is dry, nail and glue it to cabinet base, ends and partitions, checking alignment. Cut, nail and glue **AA** and **X.** Add corner blocks **BB** for securing top.

Plane or sand all facing joints flush. Cut vertical laminations to run full length of stiles; apply contact cement to mating surfaces. Butt-cut and apply end laminate. Cut and apply back laminate in one sheet. End and back edges will be covered with trim.

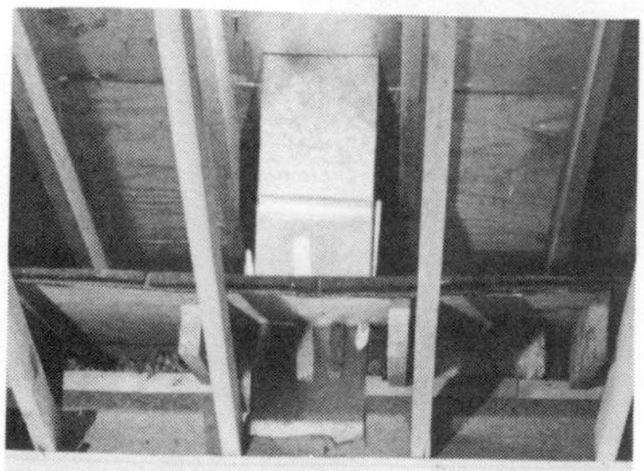

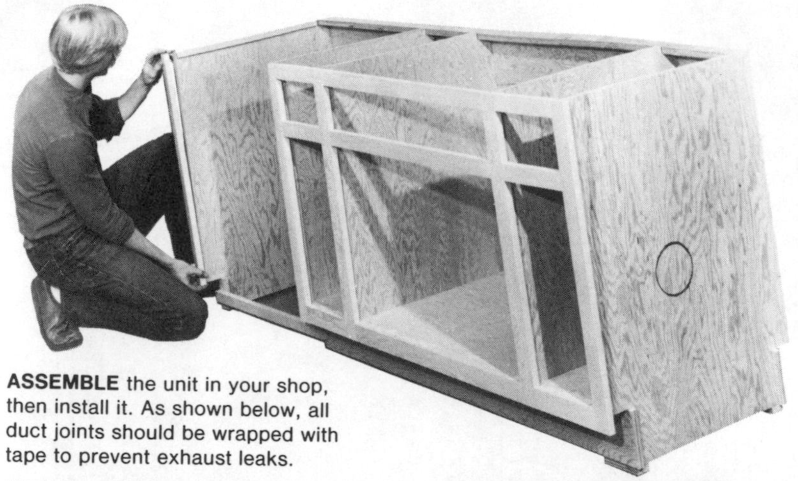

ASSEMBLE the unit in your shop, then install it. As shown below, all duct joints should be wrapped with tape to prevent exhaust leaks.

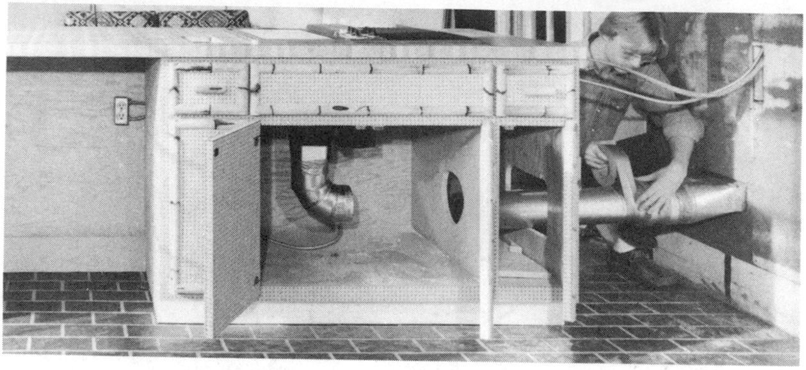

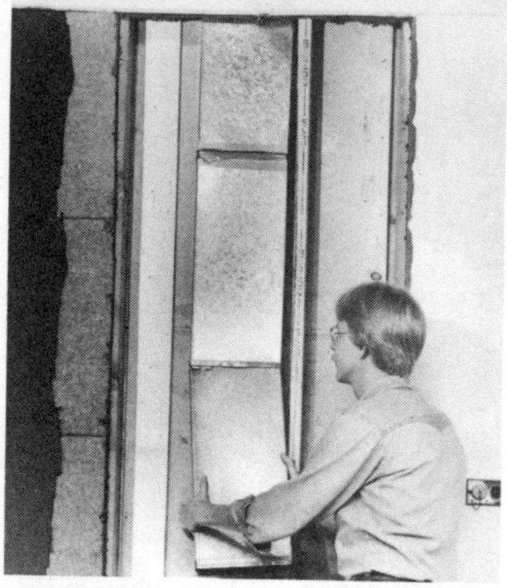

TO RETAIN effective exhaust system, use large ducts. For good air flow, use a minimum of elbows. A 5-in. elbow, 3 x 10-in. duct and roof jack worked here.

BARBECUE BAR/COFFEE TABLE—MATERIALS LIST

Key	Pcs.	Size and description	Key	Pcs.	Size and description
A	1	¾ x 29 x 80½" particleboard	R	2	¾ x 2 x 8¼" pine
B	1	¾ x 2½ x 29" plywood	S	4	¾ x 2 x 30½" pine
C	2	¾ x 2½ x 73" plywood	T	2	¾ x 6⅜ x 9⅝" plywood
D	1	¾ x 5 x 29" plywood	U	1	¾ x 6⅜ x 30¼" plywood
E	1	¾ x 29¼ x 78¼" plywood	V	2	¾ x 9⅝ x 21⅜" plywood
F	1	¾ x 5¼ x 78¼" plywood	W	2	¾ x 15 x 21⅜" plywood
G	3	¾ x 24½ x 34½" plywood	X	1	¾ x 1½ x 29¼" pine
H	2	¾ x 24½ x 28½" plywood	Y	1	¾ x 1 x 2½" pine
I	1	¾ x 24½ x 51¼" plywood	Z	1	¾ x 1½ x 5¼" pine
J	1	¾ x 5¼ x 52¾" plywood	AA	1	¾ x 1 x 22½" pine
K	1	¾ x 2 x 76¾" plywood	BB	4	¾ x 5 x 5" pine
L	2	½ x 4½ x 22¼" fir plywood	CC	1	¾ x 5 x 22" plywood
M	2	½ x 4½ x 6¼" fir plywood	DD	2	¾ x 12¼ x 22½" fir plywood
N	1	¼ x 6¾ x 22½" plywood	EE	2	¾ x 12¼ x 14¾" fir plywood
O	2	¾ x 1¾ x 28¾" pine	FF	1	¾ x 13¼ x 22½" fir plywood
P	1	¾ x 2 x 28¾" pine	GG	1	¾ x 16¾ x 26" particleboard
Q	4	¾ x 1¾ x 8¼" pine	HH	8	1¼"-dia. rattan poles

Misc.: 3 4x8 sheets plastic laminate; 1 4x8 sheet butcher block plastic laminate; 2 22-in. drawer slides; 4 magnetic catches; 4 prs. burnished brass hinges; 8d finishing nails; 4d nails; 1¼-in. No. 8 fh wood screws; 1½-in. No. 8 fh wood screws; 1¼-in. ringed nails; 1 pr. 1½-in. brass butt hinges; ⅜-in-dia. dowel; white glue, shelving hardware; contact cement, varnish or shellac.

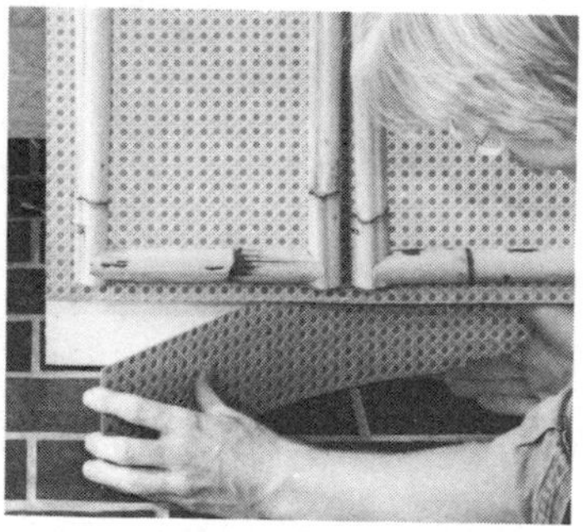

CUT AND FIT cane plastic on the kickplate with bar in position.

Lay out and cut plywood doors **T, U, V, W.** Cut laminate for door edgings (¼ in. oversize), facings and backs. (Laminate backs to guard against warpage.) Glue laminate to backs, edges and then fronts, routing edges flush after each gluing. File corners smooth.

Cut drawer sides **L** and **M.** Dado the lower edge for bottom **N.** Cut, then slide the bottom in place and attach lamination to the front. Fit piece **CC** to the cabinet and hardware to the drawer and cabinet. Screw on laminated false drawer front.

Hang the doors next. After adjusting the blade for depth, use a circular saw to cut a slot in the door for the pin hinge. Screw-fasten the hinge to the door, assemble doors to cabinet stiles and install magnetic catches.

Halve rattan **HH** or bamboo poles on the circular saw and keep matching halves together. Cut trim to length and apply it with dark areas opposite each other. Put cabinet on its back and apply vertical trim to the front with white glue and 4d finishing nails. Cope horizontal rails into the stiles. Trim outside corner with matching

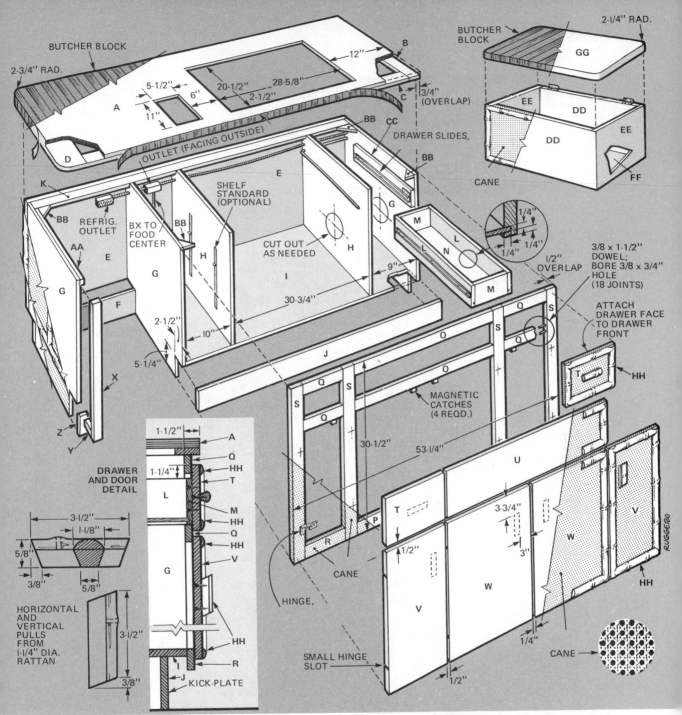

pieces. Next, lay the cabinet carefully on its face. Trim back corner with two rattan pieces. Plane the edge of the second piece for a tight fit. Add all rattan trim on the back.

Cut and install laminate facing on the refrigerator front. Add shelving if desired. Varnish the interior.

Cut countertop **A** to size. Cut reinforcing pieces **D** and **B,** glue and nail in place. Then cut and add strips **C.** Cut the corner radius with a sabre saw and sand smooth, keeping top edge square. Cut laminate self-edge slightly oversize,

bond it in place and rout the overhang flush with a straight carbide cutter in the router. File it even with the top surface. Then cut the top laminate oversize, bond it in place and dress its edges.

Bore starter holes into cutouts and complete cutouts with a hacksaw blade in your sabre saw. Rout and file all edges as needed.

Cut handles, shellac their ends and attach with 1½-in. No. 8 fh wood screws. Position barbecue bar, then cut and cement laminate to the kick-plate.

Party center bar you can build

WHEN IT'S CLOSED, no one would guess this handsome cabinet is a home bar in disguise. You'd be more apt to think it a stereo console with speakers behind the doors. When open, it's a party center with all you need to add cheer to your entertaining.

■ OPEN OR CLOSED it's a beauty. It's a bar your guests will admire every time the drinks are on the house.

True, you'll have to be able to tie the sink into a drain pipe and connect it to hot and cold-water lines, but you'll have the ultimate in a home bar. It offers a roomy storage compartment for beverages; a handy drawer for napkins, stirrers and jiggers; a colorful bar-type sink; and a built-in mini-size refrigerator.

Its cost depends on materials used. We built ours from lumbercore plywood—better plywood than common fir but more expensive. We covered the plywood with plastic laminate to add a handsome, durable finish. It, too, added to cost. We used piano-type hinges for the drop-down counter and the flip-back top. Again plain butts would cost less.

If you skip the laminate and finish your cabinet with stain and varnish, you can't get by with less than cabinet-grade, veneer-face plywood for

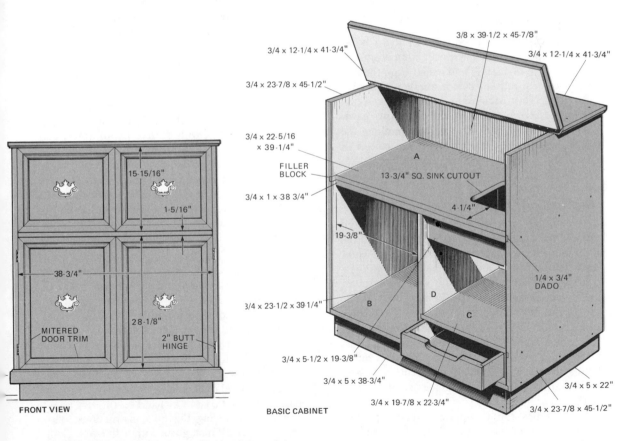

FRONT VIEW

BASIC CABINET

RECESSED SHELF between counter and doors lets you lower counter without opening doors first. The recess depth should equal the thickness of the counter plus 1/16-in. clearance. A similar clearance is allowed at top of the counter and bottom of the doors.

it to have a furniture-store finish. However, if a simulated wood-grain finish will do, you can build your bar from less expensive fir plywood.

Building the cabinet

The basic cabinet is a simple structure. A ⅜-in. plywood back sits in a rabbet; shelves A, B and C, plus partition D, rest in rabbets and dadoes. Note that the ¼ x ¾-in. blind dadoes for shelf A and partition D are cut to full panel width and later filled at the front with filler blocks. A 13¾-in.-sq. cutout is made for the sink with a sabre saw before shelf A is installed.

If you cover the plywood with laminate, it's best, and easiest, to apply it to the interior surfaces before the parts are glued and nailed. We lined the three sink-compartment walls with Chinese red and faced the counter with black slate.

To assemble your cabinet, first glue shelf C to partition D, then the partition to shelf B. Add shelf A, then the ends and the back last. Add the back temporarily for now to help brace and square-up the assembly.

Build kickboard separately

The three-piece, butt-joined kickboard is assembled separately, covered with laminate, glued to the bottom of shelf B and nailed from the top. We picked carpathian burl laminate and used it for a rich look on kickboard, ends, doors and top.

Rip the 2½-in.-wide skirt from ¾-in. hardwood, rabbet the back and run a cove along the top edge. Miter the front corners and glue it in place. The skirt is later antiqued and varnished, as is the door molding.

Add laminate before hinges

To laminate exterior surfaces: First, edge-band top and front edges of end panels before the two-piece hinged top is in place. Then face the ends. As when edge-banding, cut the laminate ⅛ in. oversize and later trim it flush with your router and a special laminate cutter or by plane and file. In positioning laminate, butt the lower edge against the skirt and place the laminate just where you want it; once the cement-coated surfaces touch, you can't shift it. Contact cement bonds instantly. The edges of partition D and shelf C are painted along with the rest of the interior.

Next comes the two-piece hinged top: The front half has a cove around three edges; the rear half has one on outside edges only. A ⅜ x ⁷⁄₁₆-in. blind rabbet is cut along the back edge for the cabinet back. Band the edges with laminate first. Keep the strips even with the cove and trim them

flush at the bottom. Cover top and bottom surfaces with laminate, but do not face the top of the rear half until it has been installed with finishing nails driven through the top into top edges of the end members. The nails will go through the banding previously cemented to the edges.

You now can cover the top surface. Try to buy a 1½-in.-wide piano hinge to join the two halves; the hinge leaves will cover the full thickness of the plywood. If you have to settle for a ¾-in. hinge, you'll need to stain the exposed wood.

Doors are like picture frames

Doors and the drop counter are ⅜-in. plywood, covered both sides with carpathian burl laminate and framed like pictures. The 1⅛-in.-thick pine molding is stocked at lumberyards as solid crown. You have to rabbet it and miter the corners. Cut the rabbet ⁷⁄₁₆ in. deep to take the added ¹⁄₁₆-in. laminate thickness. Make your frames first, insert the covered panels in the rabbets and then apply laminate to the entire backs.

The drop counter is built up quite similarly; while the frames start as two separate assemblies with inserts, they become one when glued and butted end to end. Install a drop pull in the center of each frame, with bolt heads set flush. Then cover the backs of the two frames with one piece of black slate laminate so the drop-pull screws are concealed below the surface. The counter is hinged to shelf A with a brass piano hinge, and an 18-in.-long brass support chain is attached at each end with screws. Magnetic door catches keep the counter and doors closed. The doors are hinged with 3-in. brass butts and fitted with drop pulls in antique brass. The drawer rides smoothly on two ¾-in.-wide strips of scrap laminate cemented to the bottom of the compartment along the sides.

The refrigerator compartment accommodates an RV unit which requires a 2-in. air space in back and 4 in. above. The cabinet back is permanently attached after boring holes for water and drain lines and the refrigerator cord.

We used an antiquing kit to add a chateau-walnut finish to the pine skirt and door molding.

Here's how it's applied: Prime the bare wood with an enamel undercoater. When dry, brush on base latex (first coat in kit) and let this dry about 3 hours. Following the kit's instructions, wipe on sparingly a finish glaze with a lint-free cloth. For a realistic wood-grain effect, stroke the wet glaze lightly with cheesecloth. When glaze is thoroughly dry, you can apply clear urethane for a more durable finish.

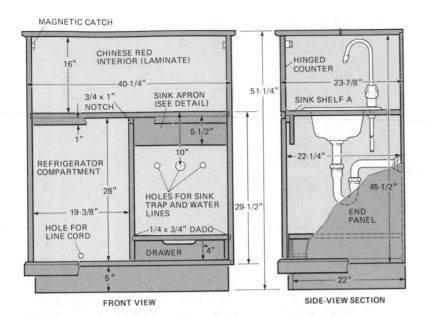

MAGNETIC CATCH

CHINESE RED INTERIOR (LAMINATE)

16"

40-1/4"

SINK APRON (SEE DETAIL)

3/4 x 1" NOTCH

1"

5-1/2"

10"

REFRIGERATOR COMPARTMENT

28"

HOLES FOR SINK TRAP AND WATER LINES

19-3/8"

HOLE FOR LINE CORD

1/4 x 3/4" DADO

DRAWER

4"

5"

FRONT VIEW

HINGED COUNTER

23-7/8"

SINK SHELF A

51-1/4"

22-1/4"

45-1/2"

29-1/2"

END PANEL

22"

SIDE-VIEW SECTION

BAR'S REFRIGERATOR compartment is dimensioned to accept this RV unit. The refrigerator has walnut-finish door and runs on a battery or 110-v. current.

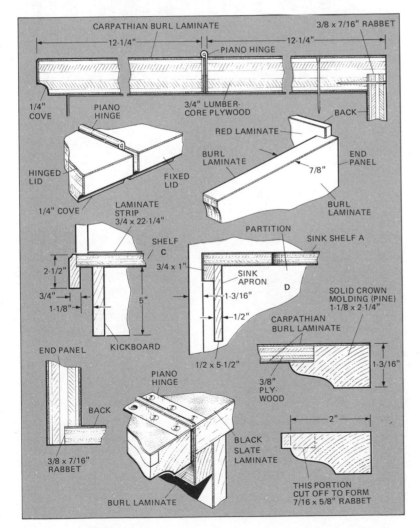

CARPATHIAN BURL LAMINATE

3/8 x 7/16" RABBET

12-1/4"

PIANO HINGE

12-1/4"

3/4" LUMBER-CORE PLYWOOD

BACK

1/4" COVE

PIANO HINGE

RED LAMINATE

END PANEL

7/8"

BURL LAMINATE

HINGED LID

FIXED LID

BURL LAMINATE

1/4" COVE

LAMINATE STRIP 3/4 x 22-1/4"

SHELF C

PARTITION

SINK SHELF A

3/4 x 1"

2-1/2"

SINK APRON

D

3/4"

1-1/8"

5"

1-3/16"

SOLID CROWN MOLDING (PINE) 1-1/8 x 2-1/4"

1/2"

CARPATHIAN BURL LAMINATE

KICKBOARD

1/2 x 5-1/2"

1-3/16"

END PANEL

PIANO HINGE

3/8" PLY-WOOD

BACK

3/8 x 7/16" RABBET

BLACK SLATE LAMINATE

2"

THIS PORTION CUT OFF TO FORM 7/16 x 5/8" RABBET

BURL LAMINATE

ACRYLIC BAR sink comes in red, black and sunflower colors with gold or chrome faucets, measures 15 x 15 in., is easy to install.

Frame a basement partition

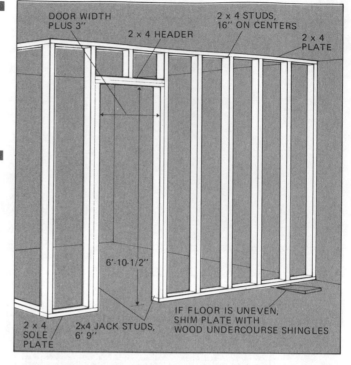

DOOR WIDTH PLUS 3"

2 x 4 HEADER

2 x 4 STUDS, 16" ON CENTERS

2 x 4 PLATE

6'-10-1/2"

IF FLOOR IS UNEVEN, SHIM PLATE WITH WOOD UNDERCOURSE SHINGLES

2 x 4 SOLE PLATE

2x4 JACK STUDS, 6' 9"

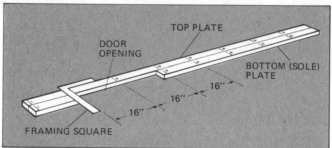

DOOR OPENING

TOP PLATE

BOTTOM (SOLE) PLATE

16"

16"

16"

FRAMING SQUARE

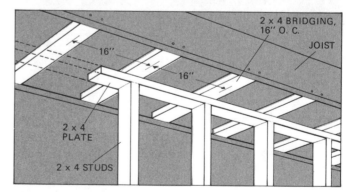

2 x 4 BRIDGING, 16" O. C.

JOIST

16"

16"

2 x 4 PLATE

2 x 4 STUDS

LAYING OUT STUDS

PARTITION WALLS can be erected by using single plates at bottom and top. Use long stock (at least 10-footers) for this chore, making certain that it's free of twist and bow. After cutting the plates to the required length, lay them side by side and mark off the stud locations (16 in. on center). Cut away portions for the door openings on the bottom plates only.

PROVIDING SOLID NAILING

IF YOUR PARTITION wall will be parallel with and between joists, you'll have to install nailers (often called cats) between—and flush with bottom of—the joists. The minimum number of nailers should be three in a 10-ft. plate-run—put one near each end and a third at the center. Cut the nailers for a force-fit between joists and install each of them with two 10-penny (10d) common nails.

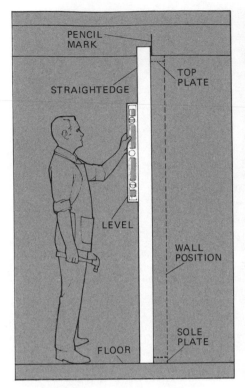

LOCATING TOP PLATE

TO SET THE WALL, snap a chalkline on the floor to mark the partition location. Then fasten the bottom plate in position, using either fluted masonry nails (wear safety goggles), lead anchors or masonry pins. To locate the top plate directly over the sole plate, use a straightedge (length of 2 x 3) and level as shown above. Plumb the straightedge and make several marks on the joists for the top plate at several points along the plate run.

BUILDING THE WALL

IF YOUR CONCRETE FLOOR is in good shape—that is, relatively level—you can assemble the studs to the top plate on the floor, then tilt the wall up into position as a unit. Check studs with your level (both vertical planes must be plumb) and fasten the top plate to joists with 10d nails spaced 16 in. o.c. But if your floor is not level, fasten the top plate only to those points marked on the joists and cut and install the studs one at a time. Stand on the sole plate to mark a stud for length, then cut the stud full (i.e., leave the line). Such a force-fit bears against the plates for rigidity; when you remove your weight, the plate springs up. You may find an assistant helpful for this part of the work.

NAILING A STUD

TO TOENAIL A STUD, place the stud on the line on the bottom plate and about an inch or so above the plate, then drive two 8d nails at about a 60° angle. Even though you buck the board (brace it with your shoe) it will move slightly off the line; bring it back to the line by driving a third 8d nail on the opposite side. Finally, to fix the stud, drive in a fourth nail on the face, or narrow, side. Repeat the toenailing at the top if installing the studs individually as mentioned under the heading *Building the wall* in the column at the right.

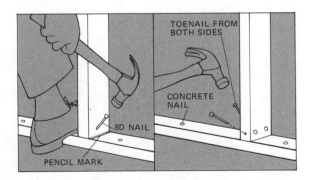

Remodeling a basement

A LONG ENTRANCE hallway separates the basement work areas. The curved wall here hides an oversize chimney.

■ DOLLAR FOR DOLLAR, the best way to add lots of living space to your home is by remodeling the basement.

A full basement provides extra room at a fraction of what home additions cost. With your imagination, and the ideas presented here, you can transform your basement into a spacious family room or a first-rate home office.

Curved wall

Although the finished side of this curved wall is concave, the same basic construction applies to a convex curve; just turn the plates around. To begin, install the floor blocking and plate as shown. From this plate, plumb up to the floor joist to position the top of the wall. Install enough blocking between the joists to provide nailing backup for the upper plate assembly. Then cover the joist with drywall, and nail in the upper blocking. Attach the plate so it's plumb in both directions with the lower one. Lay out stud positions, then measure each stud individually to accommodate any difference in length caused by an uneven floor. Install the studs plumb and attach the drywall. Most professionals dampen the back of the panels to aid in bending.

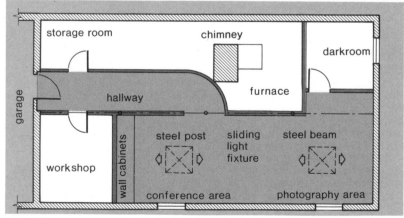

IN MOST BASEMENTS the only load-bearing member within the foundation walls is a center beam. As long as this remains properly supported, the space can be divided any way you choose. Access to rest of house in this plan is by a stairwell in the garage.

BEGIN BUILDING CURVED wall by laying out proper arc on floor, using board with pivot nail in one end and pencil at the other end. Board length should match curve radius.

CUT 2x4 STOCK into 12-in. lengths and nail to floor, using masonry nails. Keep boards back from the arc line at least ⅝ in. at the closest points. Wear eye protection.

USING THE SAME marking jig, transfer wall arc onto ¾-in. plywood. Extend jig 3½ in., then mark plywood again. Cut out stock between lines with sabre saw.

TEST-FIT BOTTOM plywood plate to be sure arcs align. Then cut plate to length and use it to trace matching plywood plate for wall top. Nail plate to 2x4 floor blocks.

NAIL 2x4 BLOCKS to ceiling and install upper plywood plate. Then measure each stud length individually, cut each to length, and toenail along arc on 12-in. centers.

MARK STUD POSITION on face of drywall panel and nail one edge to the wall. Slowly push it until middle of the sheet hits remaining studs. Maintain pressure as you nail.

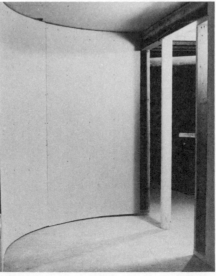

THE FINISHED curved wall, ready for taping.

FRAMING AROUND PIPES, steel beams, heat ducts and other obstructions is time-consuming but necessary to support drywall, which gives the room a finished look.

Hiding pipes

Probably the most basic problem to be faced when remodeling a basement is related to its original design. Most of these rooms were never meant to be finished living spaces—at least not in the builder's mind—and because of this, construction practices that would never pass muster in the rest of the house go unchecked.

Certainly the most annoying of these is the reduced headroom that results from shorter foundation walls. This problem is compounded by low-hanging plumbing pipes, heat ducts and, in some older homes, electrical wiring conduit—all of which should be hidden to give the room a finished look. Even though many of these com-

BEGIN FRAMING by finding the lowest point of obstruction (waste line above). Position a level furring strip at that point, and draw a line across studs at the top of the strip.

TACK-NAIL BOARD to wall stud just to under marked line and another board to floor joist as shown. Clamp together, adjust for level and plumb, then mark for cutting.

INSTALL BLOCKING between joists to provide sound nailing for frame boards. Then nail boards in place, making sure they're installed square to wall, even if pipe is not.

INSTALL FRAMEWORK side by suspending it from edge of joist-mounted boards. Make sure side is plumb, level and square to wall before nailing all boards in place.

LAST STEP IN building framework is to nail filler blocks between vertical suspension boards. This provides necessary support for installing drywall corner bead later.

DON'T COVER UP pipes or other obstructions that require servicing, such as the waste line cleanout plug above. Instead, scribe and cut framework so plug is accessible.

A T-BRACE made of 1x4 and 2x4 stock is a great help when drywalling a ceiling. Cut stud ½ in. longer than room height. Lift panel into place while a helper wedges brace under the panel.

LEAVE ADEQUATE drywall clearance around areas that require servicing, like this cleanout plug. When ceiling is finished, make wood plate to cover hole.

INSTALLING DRYWALL on a ceiling with many different surfaces requires careful preparation. Be sure you have solid nailing behind the perimeter of all sheets.

ponents could be moved up between the joists, that could cost thousands of dollars. The more sensible approach is to construct wood frames around these obstructions and then cover the framing with drywall.

One method for constructing these frames—called soffits in the building trades—is shown. Plan the work carefully, keeping in mind how the room will look when it's done. You have two primary goals: First, try to keep the number of soffits to a minimum, even if this means increasing some in size to accommodate another obstruction close by. Second, construct a soffit level, plumb and square to the basement partitions and foundation walls, even if the obstruction is not installed that way. This will give the job a clean look that lessens the impact of an uneven ceiling.

Once you've determined where you want your soffits, begin constructing them as shown. The overhead floor joists are your most important points of attachment because they will be carrying nearly all the weight. The partitions and foundation walls basically serve to stabilize the framework and to keep it square.

Another good tip: Always try to "anchor" the soffit to a wall instead of building it so it is isolated in the middle of the room. Do this even if it requires making the soffit longer or wider than it has to be. Also, be sure to construct the framework so that all inside and outside corners have solid blocking on both sides to receive the nails used to hang the ceiling drywall.

Ceiling

Gypsum board, usually called drywall in the trades, is an excellent building material for finishing basement ceilings. It's inexpensive, easy to work with, and yields the same finished look as the other ceilings in most houses. Hanging it, however, is strenuous work. A handy T-brace helps. To use it, lift a panel into place and wedge the brace underneath. This is often a two-person job, since a 4x8 sheet of drywall is not light or easy to lift and hold while you wedge the brace in place. Once the sheet is braced in place, nail it to the bottom edge of the floor joists.

Although drywall is available in various lengths, the shortest panels, 4 ft. wide by 8 ft. long, are the best for do-it-yourselfers because they are the lightest. Drywall also comes in different thicknesses. You can use ⅝-in.-thick sheets, but ½-in.-thick sheets will work if you maintain 16 in. or less between framing supports.

When hanging the panels, always keep the tapered edges on the panel sides next to each other. These slight depressions are designed to accommodate the tape and joint compound used to finish the surface later.

Any components that require servicing, such as cleanout plugs and wiring junction boxes, must remain accessible. Don't cover these with drywall. Once the ceiling is done, fashion wood plates to cover the access holes, then screw them into the framing. When taping is complete, paint the ceiling flat white to blend the many surfaces.

Finishing touches for basement remodeling

■ THOUGH MANY do-it-yourself articles make it seem that finishing a basement is a snap, it's not all that easy. It takes hard work and, more important, thorough planning before the job even starts. Framing and paneling the walls are probably the easiest parts of the job; how to handle finish details attractively is what usually stumps the average person remodeling a basement.

In most basements (particularly in older homes), many access doors and some intricate framing around pipes and stairs are called for. This sets up a good rule of thumb: Wherever possible, keep eye and dust-catching hardware to a minimum. The ideas on these pages—used by the professionals—accomplish just that.

The three "door" treatments shown can solve just about any concealment problem, yet they boast a flexibility that lets you adapt to suit a particular problem. There are two important points

WATER SHUTOFF is hidden by a panel that is practically invisible because there is no hardware. The "door" removes quickly—a feature that is a must in an emergency; two magnetic catches hold it in place and cost only pennies. To minimize the chance of ½-in. panel warping, use contact cement to glue cutout before fitting magnetic catches.

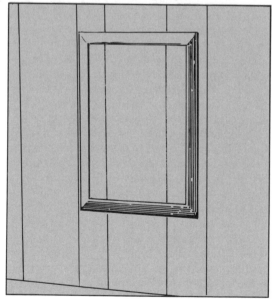

to remember: First, make sure that all access openings are framed large enough so that it will not be necessary to rip out a wall if plumbing or electrical repairs are ever needed. Second, after the framing in front of foundation walls is up, walk around the room and double-check to insure that all valves, cutoffs and the like have been provided with an adequate opening.

Though there are several methods for boxing-in a girder (ladderlike framing is perhaps the

WALL ACCESS PANEL

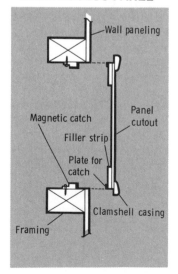

Wall paneling

Magnetic catch

Filler strip

Plate for catch

Framing

Panel cutout

Clamshell casing

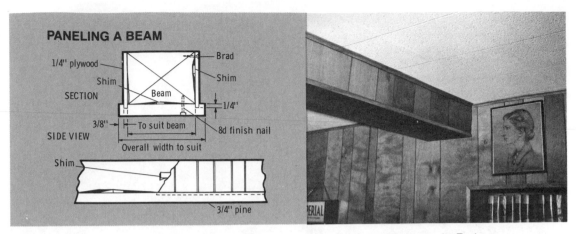

GOOD-LOOKING WAY to box in a beam eliminates time-consuming framing, costs less to do. Tack the clear pine temporarily to the beam's underside, level it with shims and drop the plywood panels into the grooves. Then, using undercourse shingles as shims, plumb the paneling, tack it at the top and nail the pine in place. Panel both sides completely before you drive the nails.

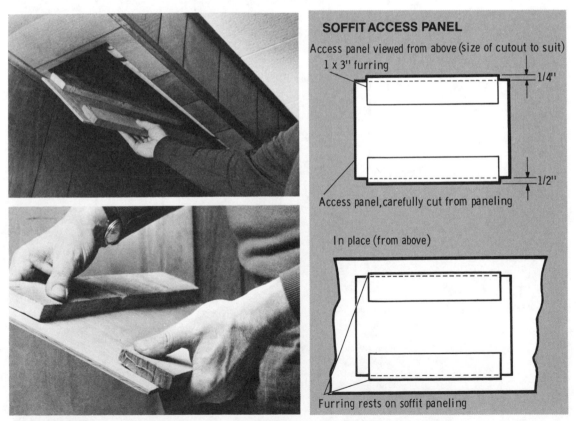

HARD-TO-SPOT access panel in box around pipes is pushed up, then lowered for removal. Here, since the joint is not concealed by molding, the panel should be cut from the drop ceiling to insure a splinterfree straightedge. Furring strips are fastened with glue and brads. Access panels shown are cut to insure a V-groove alignment between the panel and the cutout. Size depends on the opening.

most common), the technique shown is far simpler and saves materials. To insure a good-looking job, the pine on the underside should be clear.

Finally, it's a mistake to close-in both sides of the basement stairs permanently, since this restricts the size of furniture you can move in or out. Instead, finish the room side up to the top of the stringer only and build a removable frame with four or five heavy dowels (such as closet poles). If your basement has a center stairway, consider making both sides removable.

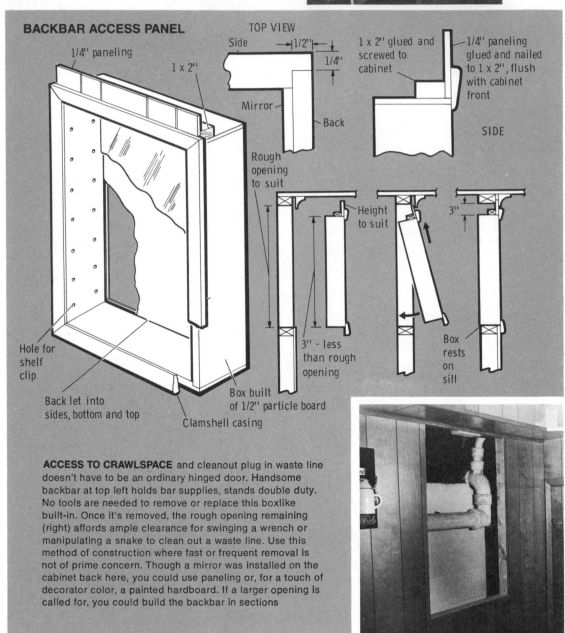

BACKBAR ACCESS PANEL

1/4" paneling

1 x 2"

TOP VIEW

Side

1/2"

1/4"

Mirror

Back

1 x 2" glued and screwed to cabinet

1/4" paneling glued and nailed to 1 x 2", flush with cabinet front

SIDE

Rough opening to suit

Height to suit

3"

3" - less than rough opening

Box rests on sill

Hole for shelf clip

Back let into sides, bottom and top

Clamshell casing

Box built of 1/2" particle board

ACCESS TO CRAWLSPACE and cleanout plug in waste line doesn't have to be an ordinary hinged door. Handsome backbar at top left holds bar supplies, stands double duty. No tools are needed to remove or replace this boxlike built-in. Once it's removed, the rough opening remaining (right) affords ample clearance for swinging a wrench or manipulating a snake to clean out a waste line. Use this method of construction where fast or frequent removal is not of prime concern. Though a mirror was installed on the cabinet back here, you could use paneling or, for a touch of decorator color, a painted hardboard. If a larger opening is called for, you could build the backbar in sections

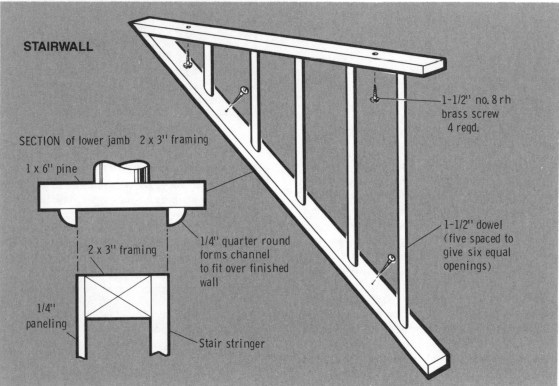

STAIRWALL

SECTION of lower jamb 2 x 3" framing

1 x 6" pine

2 x 3" framing

1/4" paneling

1/4" quarter round forms channel to fit over finished wall

Stair stringer

1-1/2" no. 8 rh brass screw 4 reqd.

1-1/2" dowel (five spaced to give six equal openings)

DOWEL TREATMENT permits light to enter from above, eliminates cavelike look found in many basements. To remove the "wall," the lowest screw through the pine frame into the stringer is last removed (above right). Stairwall should be framed and paneled first, then removable section built to fit. Quarter-round molding (above) brackets the stringer to guide the unit

Waterproof your basement

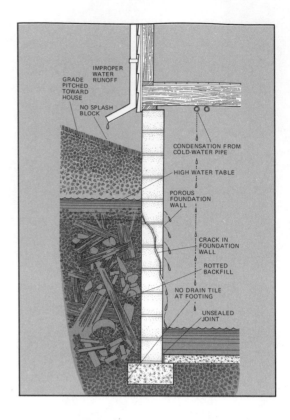

IMPROPER WATER RUNOFF

GRADE PITCHED TOWARD HOUSE

NO SPLASH BLOCK

CONDENSATION FROM COLD-WATER PIPE

HIGH WATER TABLE

POROUS FOUNDATION WALL

CRACK IN FOUNDATION WALL

ROTTED BACKFILL

NO DRAIN TILE AT FOOTING

UNSEALED JOINT

■ WHEN THE NEED for extra living space involves the basement, one thing is certain—it had better be dry. Several inches of water won't help carpeting or wall paneling, and even when it comes to setting up a workshop, a damp musty basement can cause such problems as warped lumber, tool rust, sticking doors and windows.

These four pages show you what you can do about a damp or wet basement—from simple cures for condensation to a thorough job of foundation waterproofing from the outside. Not all problems will yield to these solutions, however. You may have to install a sump pump or consider having work done by commercial waterproofers.

Commercial firms use several methods, including application of water-repellent silicones to exterior foundation walls below grade without excavation. Since commercial waterproofing is not cheap, you should shop for it just as carefully as you would for any other home improvement of comparable cost.

Your first step, though, is to study the drawing above right. It may give you a clue to the cause of a basement problem that you can solve yourself. Simply pitching the grade away from a house, for example, has dried out many a wet basement.

Why a basement isn't dry

The sketch above shows a number of problems that can contribute to making a basement wet. They include improper runoff, a high water table (prevailing level below which ground is saturated with water) and poor backfill with debris that decomposes to create water-retaining spaces in the ground.

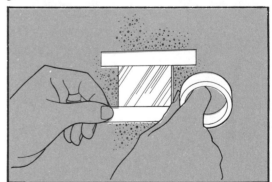

Checking for condensation

Test for condensation by taping a pocket mirror or scrap of shiny metal to the dampest wall. If this is covered with mist or water droplets after 24 hours, condensation is the problem or is contributing to a wet basement.

What to do about condensation

Insulate all exposed cold-water pipes with a good quality wrapping—fiberglass insulation (near right) or foam plastic sleeves (far right), closing slits with tape. Replace any leaking plumbing. Ventilate the basement well: Keep windows open day and night in fair weather, close them when outside air is moist. Prune or thin plantings to let a maximum of sunlight into the basement. Other steps: Do not dry clothes on a line in the basement. Make sure the clothes dryer is vented to the outside. A window airconditioner will remove some moisture from the air; some have dehumidifying cycles. Separate dehumidifiers are also available.

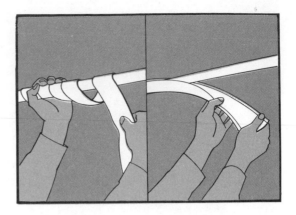

Repairing foundation cracks

Cracks in foundation walls most often occur along masonry-block joints, owing to settling. When inspecting for cracks, start at places where the foundation receives most stress—around windows, doors, and pipe and cable entries. A crack inside may mean a crack outside as well, but interior cracks should be repaired in any case, and in many instances this will complete the repair. Using a masonry or cold chisel, begin the repair by chipping out the crack, undercutting so that the crack is wider at the bottom than it is at the surface. Then rub briskly with a stiff wire brush to remove all loose particles of concrete and mortar.

With the crack prepared, it can be patched with mortar or cement. Wet the crack first; this will retard hydration and assure a strong bond between the patch and the original material. Butter the crack with patch mix, making certain that the patch is forced into every crevice. Allow the patch to cure for 2 to 3 weeks; keep it damp for at least the first 24 hours. Where water is flowing from a crack or hole, patching with quick-setting mortar may be possible; it is held tightly in place against the leak, and sets in a few minutes. Epoxy patches, applied without moistening the wall, cure in about 24 hours. With all patch mixes, follow instructions.

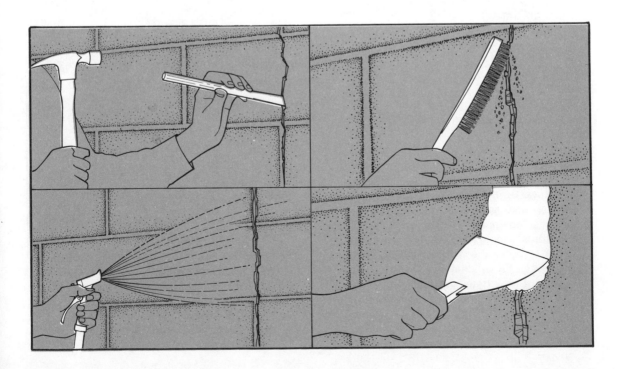

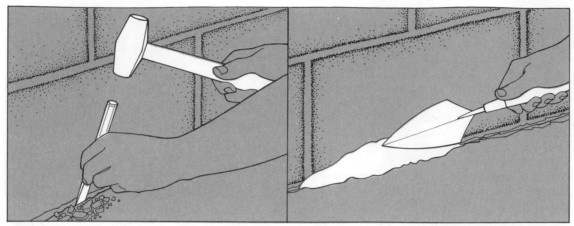

Check the wall-floor joint, too

If an unsealed or cracked joint between wall and floor is a source of water, it can be sealed with epoxy mortar. Here, too, the area to be patched or sealed is chiseled out with undercut to key the mortar in place. Loose particles, dirt and chips should be completely removed—use a whisk broom or vacuum-cleaner exhaust. Epoxy mortar is troweled on, smoothed with the oiled bowl of a cheap spoon. Hot tar is generally used to seal this joint in new construction, but it is extremely dangerous for the homeowner to attempt this indoors and is not recommended for a novice.

Interior coatings

If wetness or dampness is not caused by condensation, and remains a problem after cracks have been repaired, suspect seepage through a porous foundation wall. This is usually the result of deterioration of concrete that included too much sand in the original mix. One or—better—two coats of an interior dampproofing or waterproofing material may arrest seepage, and, although applying it is not a small job, it is much less difficult and expensive than excavating and waterproofing from the outside. Commercially available coatings are of several types—mortar, epoxy, emulsified latex—and may be sold dry or premixed. Surface preparation requirements vary. Roughening the wall may be called for, or etching with muriatic (hydrochloric) acid—if you must do this, be sure to protect your eyes and skin.

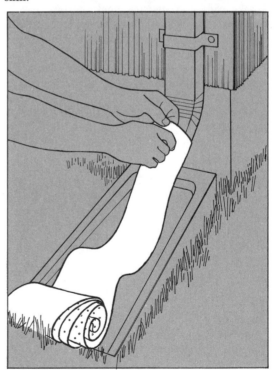

Assure good runoff

Gutters and downspouts are important protection for your basement as well as the rest of your home. To divert water from foundation walls, use a commercial plastic extension or a splash block as above. Perforated with sprinkler holes near end, the extension carries the water to lawn or plantings where it will be absorbed.

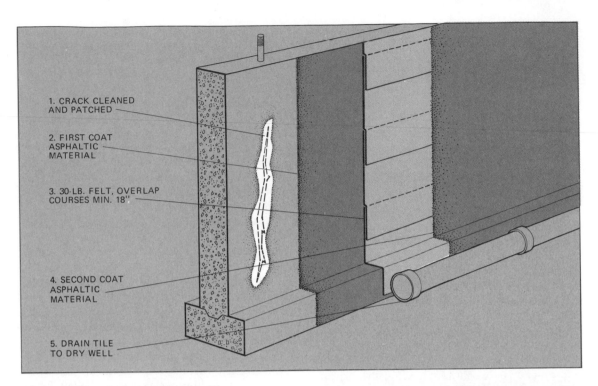

1. CRACK CLEANED AND PATCHED

2. FIRST COAT ASPHALTIC MATERIAL

3. 30-LB. FELT, OVERLAP COURSES MIN. 18"

4. SECOND COAT ASPHALTIC MATERIAL

5. DRAIN TILE TO DRY WELL

How to do exterior waterproofing

Most drastic but sometimes unavoidable is a complete exterior waterproofing job. Since this project requires excavation to the base of the wall footings, it's a lot of work, but it may be the only effective way to correct wetness.

After excavation, all visible cracks must be cleaned out and patched. Masonry-block walls that do not already have such a coating are then "parged"—given two ¼ or ⅜-in. coats of a mortar made of 1 part portland cement, 2½ parts sand. Masonry should be cleaned and moistened before parging. The first coat (often called scratch coat) is lightly roughened with a stiff brush and should not yet be firmly set when the second is applied. The second coat is steel-troweled to a smooth finish. Poured-concrete walls, like the one shown above, do not require parging.

Next, a coat of hot tar is mopped onto the wall and footing, followed by lengths of 30-lb. felt laid horizontally, each course overlapping the preceding one by a minimum of 18 in. A second coat of hot tar is then mopped on.

Drain tile should be laid along the footing, below the level of the bottom of the floor slab. Pitch the run toward a dry well, outfall or storm sewer. Bell-end tiles shown above are used where water table is high to conduct water from downspouts away from house. Where water table is low, drain tile collects water from base of

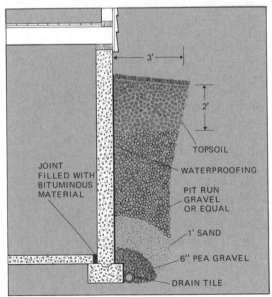

3'

2'

JOINT FILLED WITH BITUMINOUS MATERIAL

TOPSOIL

WATERPROOFING

PIT RUN GRAVEL OR EQUAL

1' SAND

6" PEA GRAVEL

DRAIN TILE

foundation and carries it off. For this purpose, short sections of tile are used, with ¼-in. gaps between sections covered with 30-lb. felt. Open tile laid this way will, over its run, lose some water to the ground.

Backfill (replacement for excavated material) should be as shown above. Grade topsoil away from house, with a minimum of 8 in. between highest grade and top of foundation. Tamp fill at each stage to minimize later settling.

Bathrooms: remodel or maintenance

■ THE FOLLOWING SECTION contains helpful information and tips so you can plan and build a better bathroom. Any house with a drab or worn-out bathroom can make you feel like moving into a new home. But with information like this, and a little time and elbow grease, you can build a new extra bathroom or renew any existing one. With new fixtures, cabinets and wallpaper, it could seem like a new house when you renovate one room! With planning for the needs of your family included, it will indeed be a new house—and you won't have to suffer the disruption of a move or the burden of heavier financial commitments.

The following pages contain ideas and information that will assist you in many aspects for the construction or remodel, or just a tune-up of your "new" bathroom.

Technical tips provide extra insight into how code requirements in bathroom construction and remodeling will help you build a safer, longer-lasting project. Highlights of electrical, plumbing and construction situations are discussed.

Faucets and fixtures shows you some new bathroom hardware features. Pictures and descriptions of the products help you make better choices at the plumbing supply store or home center.

Bathroom finishing techniques provides some insight into popular tasks that will make your bathroom look like new. Wall coverings, vinyl flooring, ceramic tile, paint and other do-it-yourself jobs are demystified.

Caulk a bathtub provides answers to a common problem in many homes. Have a look at this if you see any gaps when you sit in your tub.

Contemporary bathroom remodel shows how a house with a cramped and inadequate bathroom was transformed into a comfortable home—even if the remodel did raise the roof to do it. More space was added, making room for a shower as well as a tub, with extra light from a new skylight and windows.

Bathroom remodeling for more convenience is an account of problem-solving in an existing bathroom. It is a remodel to correct 20-year-old moisture problems, and to give a new modern look with more storage capacity.

Remodel your bath for easy care shows you how a redesign made this part of a home more efficient and much more appealing. It will now be easy to keep clean and fresh.

Prefab baths are easy to install as you can see from this do-it-yourself project. Check it out for better ideas for your new tub replacement and learn how to do it right.

Create the illusion of a sunken tub with a platform around your tub. The ideas you gain from this project could give your home an exciting new look.

Victorian bathroom deals with the installation of genuine old but renovated fixtures in a new house. With the addition of Victorian-style wallpaper, molding and wall paneling, it became a model bathroom of that historic era.

Towel racks you can make are easy workshop projects that will relieve any clutter on your bathroom walls and bring cheers from the family.

Early American shaving console offers plans for a decorative yet very functional project to bring pleasure to a close shave—while hiding the mess.

Shaving cabinets you can make are two good wall-mounted projects that will keep shaving implements out of the way but ready for service.

Plumbing is the topic of a major section in Volume 19. There you'll find help in unclogging drains as well as working with pipe and fixtures in your bathroom.

More how-to-do-it help

You can get more information to help you from several sources. Many manufacturers provide information with product displays in retail stores so you will feel more comfortable installing their faucets or tubs. Most provide installation checklists and precise measurement guides with the product.

Owner-builder classes are a good source of additional help for the amateur or do-it-yourselfer who wants hands-on experience before bringing the crowbar into the bathroom at home. These are available at schools and adult education programs all over the country. They offer classes and actual practice in all aspects of house building and home maintenance. Most programs offer weekend and evening courses as well as longer projects in summer school.

A FRESH new bathroom can make your home more usable and feel like a new house without buying one.

Technical tips

■ **MODERN CODE REQUIREMENTS** are quite specific about the details of bathroom remodel projects. Rather than being considered a burden, these recommendations should be followed carefully to keep your family safe and make your "new" bathroom a long-lasting success. After all, codes are the result of extensive testing combined with observation from experience that is shaped into rules and procedures guaranteed to work and last. For example, plumbing that doesn't leak and electrical wiring that can't kill have been developed and are required by code. These are conditions everyone should want in a home.

Remodel by the rules

Today it is even easier to do things right. Most home supply stores sell products that have been engineered and produced to code requirements by the factory. Salespeople generally give you only products that are compatible with the code for the project at hand. Any up-to-date manual will point out the best procedures for general code compliance. Finally, it is up to you to look for help when your job puzzles you. And that help is nearby. Every town has a building department with a staff drawn from experienced tradespeople. You should always discuss your project with these officials before you begin or even buy materials. Frequently, local building ordinances have special requirements based on local conditions. These procedures may differ from state or national codes. The only way is the right way for where you live. The building inspector can suggest specific materials to purchase and tell you how best to install them. If you arrange for inspections, you will gain the security of knowing you did everything right. In some

GROUND FAULT CIRCUIT INTERRUPTERS will protect you and your family from serious electrical shock.

cases, if problems occur in uninspected work, your home insurance will be voided and no claims will be paid!

Electrical highlight

Electrical wiring procedures are extremely important to follow precisely. Shocks or fire can result from ignorance or shoddy workmanship. Because of grounding water pipes and wet surfaces in any bathroom, electrical problems can be fatal. Yet bathroom wiring is not very complicated; lights are generally built into walls or ceiling with only a switch or two, and one outlet can handle the hair dryer or electric razor.

To prevent shocks, electrical codes require the

installation of *ground fault circuit interrupters* (*GFCI*). These devices turn off any electric line automatically and instantly if the slightest overload is sensed. The GFCI can be wired into an existing or new bathroom circuit either as a breaker at the main panel or as the receptacle at each outlet.

Plumbing notes

Plumbing expense and trouble will be minimized if you don't have to move any pipes in your bathroom remodel. If possible, try and retain fixtures in the same location. When you reuse a tub or sink, you save the cost of a new one and the effort of replumbing it. On the other hand, your bathroom may not have a new look and better utility unless you do swap the old tub for the new one-piece tub and shower combination. Just attempt to use the same drain and supply lines where you can.

While in the remodeling process, plan for future maintenance of the bathroom. Change or replace any plumbing parts that are not in excellent condition. Add shutoff valves to every water line supplying any fixture. Many older houses were plumbed with only one water shutoff, usually "conveniently" located in a dark corner of the basement or in a vault in the yard. Modern plumbing code requires valves by the end use point of every line so that you don't have to run to the basement to change a washer in the third floor bath sink or hunt for a hidden valve when a fixture springs a leak.

Switch to plastic pipe where it is permitted by code. Plastic pipe requires fewer tools to work, is easy and quicker to install by the do-it-yourselfer, and will last many times the life of metal pipes.

Save water. Install flow restrictor washers in faucets and showerheads, or switch to new units with water-saving design. Older fixtures use much more water than is required. Waste costs you money in energy to heat and money for the water itself. It also burdens sewage disposal sysems. Many toilets from quality manufacturers are also now designed to use as much as 60% less water. Install one if you can.

Construction tips

Lack of proper ventilation is the cause of most rot or decay problems in old bathrooms. Most people close doors and windows when they bathe or shower, causing moisture to accumulate. Built-in vents with automatic fans connected to the outside can dissipate the moisture, and dramatically improve the life of a bathroom. Hide the vent pipe inside construction when you redo the wall or ceiling. Add the switch so it can be turned on when anyone enters the bathroom. The vent itself is a box permanently mounted in the ceiling. This box contains the fan and fan motor in simple models while fancy units may have a light and heat lamp as well.

Use water-resistant construction materials wherever possible. Plywood, for floors or walls, should be exterior grade because it is made with waterproof glue. It will resist delamination if any leaks do occur. Any plasterboard must be the water-resistant type, easily identified by its greenish surface. Gaps between plumbing fixtures should be sealed with plumber's putty or special silicone caulking material, as specified by the manufacturer's instructions.

Additional or built-in storage is another aim of many bathroom projects. Plan these aspects carefully, making sure that doors, shelves or drawers will be located with sufficient operating room. Many medicine or vanity cabinets are designed to recess into the wall cavity. When you add one of these, plan the niche carefully to be in the precise location and clear of any pipes or electrical cables.

Storage can be expanded with wall-mounted cabinets or shelving as well. You can also install larger cabinets to hold towels, linen or bath clothes. Remember to construct any unit with strong back plates or attachment braces and to evaluate your proposed wall for hanging any cabinet. The most secure fasteners are screws or lag bolts that connect into wall studs. If you must attach anything to plaster or gypsum wallboard, use only toggle bolts or metal fasteners of the size rated for the weight of the project and the kind of wall. Follow this same procedure for attaching permanent shelving. Sometimes a good choice is wall-mounted standards with adjustable shelf brackets.

If your bath is a large room or your floor plan can be made compact, you might consider erecting permanent partition walls on one side or in a corner, which will give you a regular linen closet as well as a refurbished bathroom. Follow standard construction code, and use water-resistant materials wherever possible.

Many new bathrooms include an area with washer and dryer. Since plumbing and electrical systems can be modified during a remodel, it is a good time to add this feature to a home. Washers and dryers require their own separate electrical lines, and dryers should be vented to the outside. Follow code for these electrical and plumbing hookups.

Faucets and fixtures

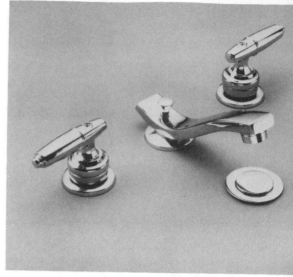

A CHROME AND BRASS faucet gives a clean new look if your design is traditional.

■ IN MOST CASES, if you want a new look in your bathroom, you will want to change the fixtures and many of the faucets you have now.

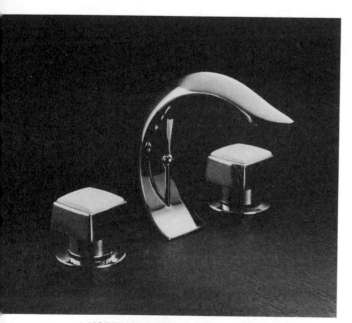

A MODERN FAUCET like this one will jazz up any bathroom project.

Faucets

Chrome is no longer the only color for faucets, and their shape can vary from Louis XIV to Buck Rogers. The variety seen in a visit to a residential plumbing supply house or large home center store should satisfy—or confuse—anyone. Just a couple of examples are shown here to give you an idea of the choices. Most faucets today come with one spout that mixes hot and cold water when you turn each knob. That spout can be plain or fancy in a decorator style, or a tall loop for more convenience. There is a variety of knobs to control the water. Simple plated knobs come with the basic faucet, but there are more options at higher prices: plastic that looks like crystal, polished brass, porcelain with painted designs, synthetic stone and even precious metal plating. The finish of the faucet can be shiny (polished), dull (satin), or glazed (antiqued). Your job is to choose tub and basin faucets of a shape, color and design that will match or combine well with the colors and styles of your other fixtures, wallpaper and general paint scheme. While this may seem like a headache at the store, careful coordination will give you a reason for genuine pride. Remember to buy name brand, quality faucets. Close-outs are a good bargain only if replacement and repair parts are readily available. Before purchase, double-check that the particular faucets you have chosen will fit the fixtures. Adaptors or modifications sometimes work, but don't wait to find out until you are underneath the sink to discover the threads won't match the hole.

Apart from the array of variety in faucets, there has been real improvement in function. Space age materials in the operating valves allow new faucets to operate for years without maintenance. O-rings instead of washers give longer service. Flow-restricting designs help you save money by retarding water waste. If your bathroom project does not include water-saving faucets, you can add flow-restricting washers to most in a jiffy. New water-saving shower heads should be added or included in even the simple bathroom remodel.

Bathtubs

Tubs are no longer just big lumps of cast iron for a hot bath. Fiberglass units of all sizes and shapes can include a shower and even underwater hydrojets for relaxation or therapy. Fiberglass is much lighter so it is easier to install. It can be formed in one-piece units for leakproof operation. Other fiberglass systems provide tub enclosures for an existing tub to give a new look to a remodel. Many let you add a shower to the old tub. If you plan carefully, you can have a "new" bathroom just for the cost of this equipment and your time to install and decorate.

A new line of bathtubs are spa baths or hot tubs. These are large tubs that will accommodate more than one person and are used as much for relaxation and therapy as for bathing. Spas are made in many shapes in fiberglass and are available fixed in a permanent location inside your home or portable for deck or yard. The fixed units have sophisticated plumbing, with pumps and hydrojets. Their final installation should be assigned to a dealer or professional plumber for best results. The portable type may weigh up to 300 lbs. or more, so you may want to move it only seasonally. They have self-contained pumps and heaters, so you just fill it with water and plug in to a properly wired outside electrical outlet. With a lift-off cover and heavy insulation, the water will stay hot for many hours, allowing a summer private bath in the great outdoors.

Toilets

Toilets don't have to be drab anymore. They are available in designer colors to coordinate with other plumbing fixtures, hardware or wall coverings. You can choose anything from a conventional style to a modern design that looks more like sculpture. More importantly, most units are engineered to work more efficiently and waste less water.

THIS BATH AND WHIRLPOOL could add extra relaxation and style to any remodel.

EVEN TOILETS don't have to be hidden because they're drab and dull.

Bathroom finishing techniques

THE OLD BATHROOM had outdated fixtures, worn floors, shabby walls and a tired look. The photo on the right shows the same room renovated and revitalized with ceramic tile, fresh wallpaper and new

■ THE BATHROOM IS THE ROOM that works hardest in every home. Its surfaces must be durable to stand up to the heavy use that people expect. But there is a bigger villain that many people don't even see—*moisture.*

Moisture besieges most bathrooms. Bathing in tub or shower, or just washing your hands and face, produces quantities of water vapor that sits on trim and wants to escape into wall and ceiling surfaces. Water spills from tub or basin test floors and joints every day. While good venting is essential to prevent rot and mildew on surfaces and inside walls and floors, the best defense is to use or install quality water-resistant materials. Consider the following when planning any bathroom project.

Ceramic

Ceramic tile, formerly seen only on floors and around tubs or showers, is now being used successfully on all bathroom surfaces. Countertops or vanities and walls as well as floors can be permanently finished with this durable and easy-to-clean material. Tile manufacturers offer a wide variety of colors, patterns and sizes for any period or contemporary setting. No longer does ceramic tile have to make you think of a locker room. Two factors are important to remember: Grouting joints must be treated with a silicone sealer for permanent waterproofing. Purchase only quality tile; cheap tile can be brittle and its waterproof surface may fail.

Vinyl

Vinyl, in wallpaper or floor covering, is also a good choice for a durable, permanent finish to walls and floors. Vinyl wallpaper resists water vapor and will prevent deterioration of plaster by keeping moisture out of your walls. It can also be washed easily with a damp sponge and mild detergent. For a solid bond during application, it is necessary to use a special adhesive for some brands. Check when you purchase the wallpaper

fixtures. Without major structural changes transformation was accomplished, at modest cost. The feeling is country with the addition of a few antiques and the red hexagonal tiles.

apply as you must measure and cut large pieces with accuracy. But the result is a seamless floor that is easy to clean, permanent, and virtually leakproof.

The important thing to remember with any tile or sheet flooring project is that the old floor must be flat, without holes, gaps or cracks. Any imperfections in the old surface will show in the soft new vinyl and cause that spot to wear prematurely. If you have any doubt about the strength and surface of the old floor, pull it up and install waterproof plywood or particleboard subflooring. If the floor is sound but the surface is pitted and irregular, nail down a new surface of tempered hardboard. Then lay down the new vinyl, carefully following the manufacturer's directions.

Paint

Paint is sorely tested in the bathroom. Moisture in the wood attempts to prevent it from a good bond to start with, and droplets of condensation fight to penetrate it later on. Repainting with hasty preparation is common because the bathroom is always in demand. But a poor paint job can spoil all the time and effort of the bigger job, so take extra care to do it right. Make sure wood and plaster surfaces are completely dry and clean of grime or dust. Paint any bare spots with primer. Sand carefully with medium-grit paper or steel wool. Putty holes and cracks. Dust with a tack rag before painting and choose a dry, warm day. For best results use oil-base (alkyd) paint and apply at least two coats. A strong paint membrane can resist moisture and look great. Quality paint and careful application will keep you from having to return to the bathroom with the paint brush for a long time.

Wood

New wooden moldings and trim can dress up a plain bath or add extra design details to a bath remodel project. Check through the displays of decorative molding at your local lumberyard. A cornice molding will make any room seem more distinctive. Wooden paneling on a wall can create a Colonial period feeling, and wood on the bottom half of a wall is quite Victorian. Be sure to prime or finish any wood on both sides before fastening it in place.

The use of water-resistant materials and some decorative features will make your "new" bathroom a special place. Plan your project carefully with detailed sketches of the result you expect. With quality materials and the time for good craftsmanship, anyone can do a fine job and be proud of it.

and then follow good paper hanging practice. Make certain to select more than enough wall covering because later purchases, even of the same brand and type, may not match.

Vinyl flooring is available in sheets from long rolls, up to 12 feet wide, and as tiles of different sizes and shapes. Vinyl tile offers a wide variety of styles and colors and is easy to apply. Many brands are available with a self-stick backing that doesn't require any additional application of adhesive. Sheet vinyl is slightly more difficult to

Caulk a bathtub

■ EVENTUALLY, an annoying crack may develop where the top of your bathtub meets the wall tile. It's usually the result of slight sagging due to weight changes after repeated filling and emptying of the tub. This unsightly crack permits water to seep in, deteriorating the wall and loosening the tiles.

The solution is to fill the crack with a flexible, waterproof caulking compound. Be sure to use the type made for sealing the joint around tubs—not the kind sold for exterior house caulking. Such tub caulking comes in squeeze tubes or disposable cartridges for use in a caulking gun. It's white in color, dries quickly.

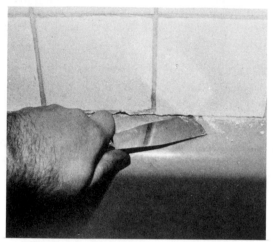

OLD CAULKING must be removed completely or it will deteriorate and affect the life span of the new caulk. Using a stiff-bladed putty knife, gouge out the caulking along the seam between the tile and the tub. This work must be done very carefully to avoid damage to both the tile and the enamel on the tub.

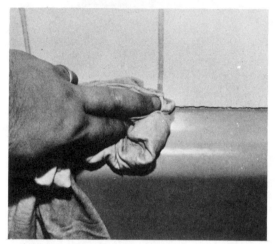

THOROUGHLY CLEAN the seam and adjacent areas to remove all dust, grime and soap film. Even a trace of residue will hinder adhesion of the caulking compound. Cleaning should be done with alcohol or another cleaning solvent. The caulk line should then be rinsed clean with water and allowed to dry thoroughly.

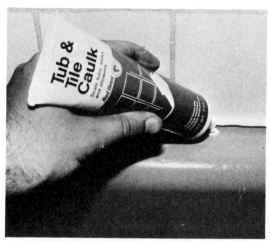

APPLY THE NEW CAULKING in a long, unbroken bead. The bead should be slightly wider than the open joint. The plastic applicator tip on the tubes of some caulking compounds such as the one shown in the photo above have gradations to provide a cutoff guide to obtain the correct bead thickness for the job.

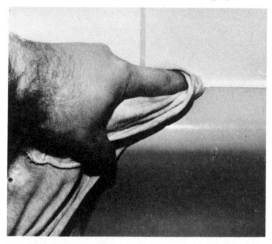

THE BEAD OF CAULK can now be worked or forced into the opening. Moisten your finger with water or wrap a cloth tightly around a finger and push the caulk firmly into the joint. With the type of caulking shown, the excess caulk can be wiped off the tile and tub with a wet cloth. Allow the caulk to dry thoroughly before painting.

Contemporary remodel

■ SOMETIMES YOU HAVE TO REMOVE A WALL TO create a larger space in an area of the house. Or you might put up a partition in a larger room to get two spaces of the proper size. In this case neither of those alternatives could be done, so without getting angry, the architect of this project raised the roof.

The original bathroom

The big problem of the house was its tiny bathroom. Constructed during the last century, the house probably was designed before indoor plumbing was a common feature. Typical of old homes, the kitchen was in a connected back wing so that in case of a cookstove fire, you had a chance of saving the main building. The only bathroom was an afterthought jammed into part of the attic over the kitchen wing. Entrance is from the second floor hall by the bedrooms. It was cramped and dark without enough headroom. The house itself is small so you could not use another room for a better bathroom without losing space needed for other purposes.

The remodeling project

The best solution was to raise the roof above the bathroom and make it into a taller, larger room with dormer windows and a skylight. This was no small undertaking; the job required many days of carpentry, plumbing and other house-building skills. But now the house is more comfortable to live in, and the bathroom is a delightful place to wash, dress, or just brush your teeth.

The project began with hammers, saws and crowbars as the roof was disconnected. When it was completely detached, jacks lifted it up to its new position. New sidewalls were constructed and nailed into place for support. Windows and skylight were installed in new rough openings. Because the old roof shingles were worn out and because much new flashing needed to be added, a whole new composition shingle roof surface was installed at this time. Clapboard siding to match the main building finished the exterior. Now work could move inside to complete the interior.

SKILLED HELP may have to be enlisted or subcontracted for a complex project like this. When the structure of the new addition is closed in with walls and siding, the building is secure and work can progress on the many tasks inside.

WHAT HAD BEEN a cramped little room about the size of a closet is now a spacious and comfortable bathroom. Before it was dark and unfriendly; now a skylight and windows provide ample light. A tile shower and much-needed storage was added.

Because old fixtures were moved to new locations on the expanded bathroom floor and a tile shower added, new drain and water supply lines were plumbed into the floor. Modern lighting and electrical outlets were installed at this stage, protected by a ground fault circuit interrupter breaker. This breaker is now required by code for all bathrooms. It prevents dangerous shocks and is very important for any wet areas of a house. With rough plumbing and electrical circuits installed, plasterboard wall surfaces and a hard-wood floor were completed. Then fixtures and trim moldings could be attached in their permanent positions. The bathroom was completed with paint and wallpaper.

As you can see, this was a complicated project, but the best solution where ordinary approaches would not work. It is not the type of project for a casual do-it-yourselfer, but anyone with good carpentry skills should be encouraged to try more complex construction and a bit of imagination in similar situations.

Bathroom remodeling for more convenience

■ THE BATHROOM in a 20-year-old home can have numerous design problems that trigger a total renovation. One of the most annoying problems is the lack of adequate storage cabinets for towels, linens and toiletries. Of even greater and more serious concern is the location of windows—often placed squarely over the bathtub. Leaks in any bathroom window can severely damage walls.

You can begin renovation in a bathroom like this by closing the drafty window. Install an ex-

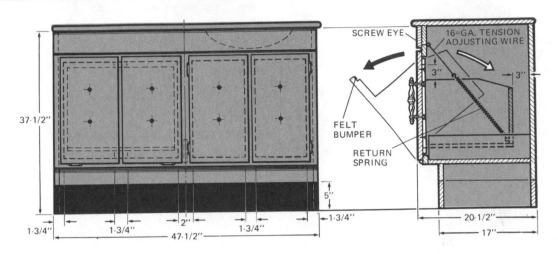

37-1/2"

5"

1-3/4" 1-3/4" 2" 1-3/4" 1-3/4"

47-1/2"

SCREW EYE

16=GA. TENSION ADJUSTING WIRE

3" 3"

FELT BUMPER

RETURN SPRING

20-1/2"

17"

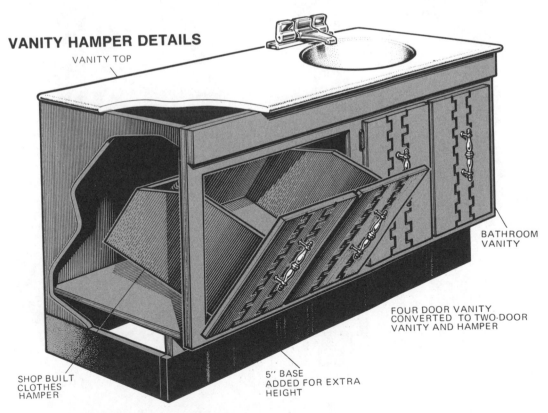

VANITY HAMPER DETAILS

VANITY TOP

BATHROOM VANITY

FOUR DOOR VANITY CONVERTED TO TWO-DOOR VANITY AND HAMPER

SHOP BUILT CLOTHES HAMPER

5" BASE ADDED FOR EXTRA HEIGHT

haust fan in its place to take care of humidity. The fan (with heat lamp) is wired to turn on automatically with the overhead light. To conceal the ductwork leading from the exhaust fan, install a suspended ceiling. After replacing any rotted studs and plasterboard that may have been damaged by leaking moisture from the window, cover the walls with Corian, a man-made plastic material that looks and feels like marble but with an important difference: It can be worked with carpentry tools so the do-it-yourselfer can easily install it. This covering provides a maintenance-free waterproof room for years to come.

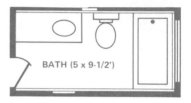

BATH (5 x 9-1/2')

TOWEL AND UTILITY CLOSET

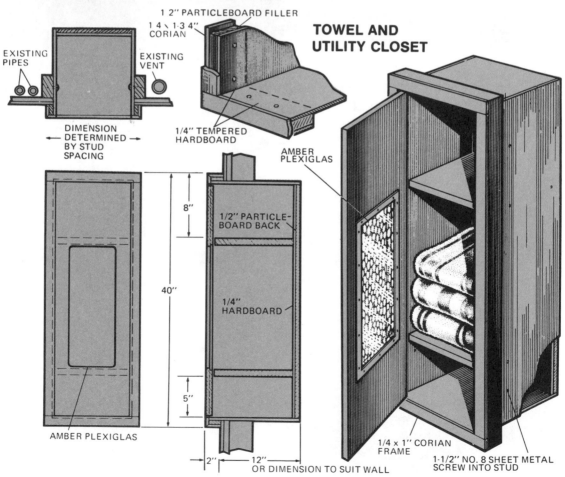

1 2" PARTICLEBOARD FILLER

1 4 \ 1·3 4" CORIAN

EXISTING PIPES

EXISTING VENT

DIMENSION DETERMINED BY STUD SPACING

1/4" TEMPERED HARDBOARD

AMBER PLEXIGLAS

8"

1/2" PARTICLE-BOARD BACK

40"

1/4" HARDBOARD

5"

AMBER PLEXIGLAS

2" — 12"

OR DIMENSION TO SUIT WALL

1/4 x 1" CORIAN FRAME

1-1/2" NO. 8 SHEET METAL SCREW INTO STUD

As you look at the pictures of the renovation here, you will see that the bath has been completely rebuilt from top to bottom; the only fixture remaining from the original room is the tub. The new vanity comes prefinished with a one-piece top and bowl; it was altered slightly to provide an out-of-sight clothes hamper.

The towel closet is built of Corian and Plexiglass, and the medicine cabinet is skinned with walnut laminate.

You can use the remodeling ideas and newer materials shown in this bathroom project to begin to plan to remodel yours.

The towel closet is built of Corian and Plexiglas, and the medicine cabinet is skinned with walnut laminate.

You can use the remodeling ideas and newer materials shown in this bathroom project to begin to plan to remodel yours.

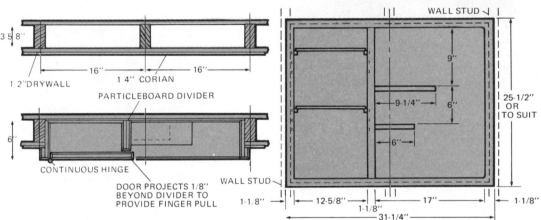

MEDICINE CABINET

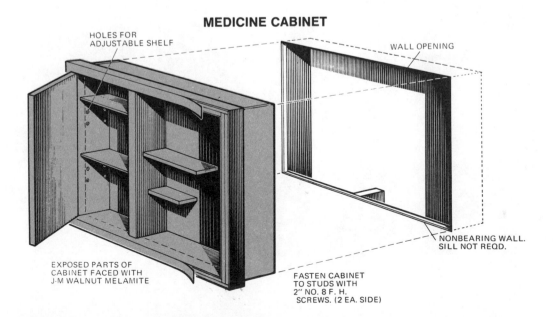

Remodel your bath for easy care

■ A LOT OF BATHROOMS are designed to look nice, but few are built for easy maintenance. In our remodeling project shown here, easy care is built into the design. It was obvious that the shiny new installation would look great in the beginning, but we wanted it to stay that way over the years with minimum cleaning. Here's how we went about eliminating those

EASY-CLEANING TILES on the vanity are recessed in the wall. In a small bathroom you need all the floor space you can get. The white, dry-cure grout is sealed with liquid silicone. Combined with a crystalline finish on tiles, it forms a waterproof barrier.

nooks and crannies that can trap dampness, germs and dirt that make a bathroom look old before its time.

The first job was a real pleasure—getting rid of the old fixtures, cracked vinyl tile and wallpaper.

Underneath this old skin were mildew, stains and soft spots from years of typical bathroom spills and splashes—not a good foundation for the new fixtures and tile. So we went farther. Old, moisture-ridden wallboard was easy to pull off the studs and the water-logged plywood sub-floor came up in pieces. We replaced insulation batts that had settled in the outside wall with new 3½-in. foil-backed fiberglass insulation.

With the walls totally open, it was a simple matter to run a new BX cable for the built-in light

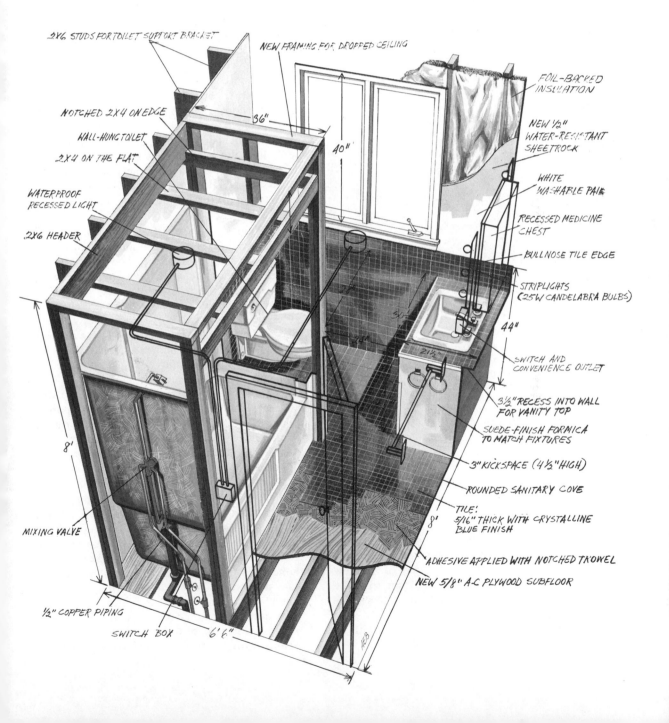

2X6 STUDS FOR TOILET SUPPORT BRACKET

NEW FRAMING FOR DROPPED CEILING

FOIL-BACKED INSULATION

NOTCHED 2X4 ON EDGE

WALL-HUNG TOILET

2X4 ON THE FLAT

WATERPROOF RECESSED LIGHT

2X6 HEADER

36"

40"

NEW ½" WATER-RESISTANT SHEETROCK

WHITE WASHABLE PAINT

RECESSED MEDICINE CHEST

BULLNOSE TILE EDGE

STRIPLIGHTS (25W CANDELABRA BULBS)

44"

SWITCH AND CONVENIENCE OUTLET

21½"

3½" RECESS INTO WALL FOR VANITY TOP

SUEDE-FINISH FORMICA TO MATCH FIXTURES

3" KICKSPACE (4½" HIGH)

ROUNDED SANITARY COVE

TILE: 5/16" THICK WITH CRYSTALLINE BLUE FINISH

ADHESIVE APPLIED WITH NOTCHED TROWEL

NEW 5/8" A-C PLYWOOD SUBFLOOR

8'

8'

MIXING VALVE

½" COPPER PIPING

SWITCH BOX

6'6"

THE ONE-PIECE TUB AND SHOWER enclosure is made of fiberglass. The smooth surface has many advantages: no hard corners, no seams or joints to crack, and the whole installation is a one-step operation. The off-white color is called "parchment."

exterior-grade plywood down to make a new subfloor. Rough carpentry included adding two 2×6 studs at the corner of the room to give extra support for the steel hanger that carries the weight of the wall-hung toilet. We measured the rough opening for the new tub and shower enclosure and framed a 3-ft.-wide 2×4 partition to separate tub from toilet. Using 2×4s on the flat, we framed a dropped ceiling over the enclosure.

For the new skin for the bath we re-covered all walls with ½-in. moisture-resistant sheetrock. You can identify this special board at the lumberyard by its light green color. Its surface is ideal for ceramic-tile installations. A three-coat taping job completed the new surfaces.

We wanted a one-piece, fiberglass tub and shower unit. The only problem was how to get it into the room. The existing door was 32 in. wide; the tub, 34 in. wide. Although it meant removing the door and jamb, getting the maintenance-free unit into the bathroom was definitely worthwhile. There are no hard corners on the smooth, glossy-surfaced enclosure; no seams to caulk, no tiles to fall off the walls and no nooks and crannies to collect dirt.

Our unit is in a new off-white color called parchment. We opted for this more subdued tone and added color with the tile, shower curtain and towels. It's easy to change if you tire of the color, but fixtures are there to stay.

The only other fixture to install was the vanity. We saved space here by recessing the vanity in the stud wall 3½ in. Front and side were covered with a suede-finish laminate colored like the fixtures. We used the paper template supplied to make the vanity-top cutout.

We chose a crystalline-finish, deep blue tile. Although you can find less expensive imported tiles, in general they are not as uniform in finished size as American-made tiles. Even seams from one end of the bath to the other are essential for appearance.

First we established the tile height on the walls. For convenience, adjust height to accommodate the nearest full tile. We used a bullnose-edged tile to form the top border and a rounded cove tile at the base. We started work on the walls by spreading 3 or 4 square feet of adhesive with a notched trowel and placing the tiles next to each other with a firm press of the hand.

A durable finish is achieved with a two-step process. First, force the dry-cure grout into the seams with a rubber-coated trowel. Several

over the new tub enclosure. Good access also made it possible to solder a copper cap onto the toilet waste drain below the floor and extend the line to meet the in-the-wall drain of the new wall-hung toilet. (This is a good time to snake through your drains to avoid septic blockages later.)

After we coated beams and sills with a moisture-resistant sealer, we laid ⅝-in. A-C

A GOOD-LOOKING VANITY

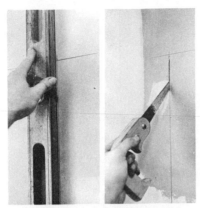

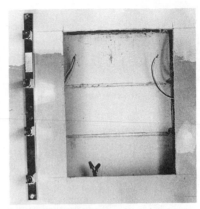

PENCIL IN THE CUT LINES for the medicine chest with the aid of a level. Cut with a keyhole saw

LIGHT STRIPS flanking the chest are wired to a junction box above the opening. Use wire nuts on all splices

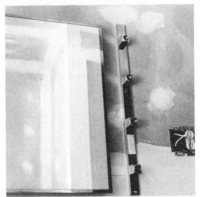

Soft light, 25-watt bulbs throw an even light on the vanity. Install a grounded receptacle next to the switch

We used a noncorroding PVC trap and copper tubing to connect the old pipes and new sink as shown above

AN EASY-MAINTENANCE, WALL-HUNG TOILET

The wall-hung toilet is supported by a steel hanger. Drill holes for the bolts and remove enough tile for the waste drain connection. A plastic sleeve will protect the fixture as the threaded bolts pass through the wall.

Careful layout is essential for proper alignment of the bolts and the openings in the hanger. If your measurements aren't exactly right, you can loosen the bolts to the 2x6s and insert shims

EASY-CARE TILE

ESTABLISH THE WALL HEIGHT and lay out dry tiles to check it. We recessed the vanity 3½-in. into the wall

SPREAD THREE SQUARE FEET OF ADHESIVE at a time with a trowel and press each tile into place firmly

MOST LOCAL TILE SUPPLIERS can rent you a cutter and chippers. After you score the surface, the tile snaps

A COVED BASE eliminates one more hard-to-clean crack. Make sure no nailheads protrude from the plywood floor

APPLY THE GROUT LIBERALLY forcing it into the seams by making continuous passes with a rubber-coated trowel

A WINDOW WASHER'S SQUEEGEE is ideal for removing the excess grout. A rag removes the final film

passes over the same area will compact the grout. Don't worry about the excess. A window washer's squeegee will remove it. Follow this with a damp sponge; it will remove all but a fine film which can be "polished" away with a dry rag.

The following day we finished the tile job by brushing a liberal coating of liquid silicone on the grouted joints. This is tedious, but it will save you hours of maintenance.

Two coats of washable latex paint completed the resurfacing of our modern, efficient bath. The thorough installation will keep it looking good with a minimum of effort.

Prefab baths are easy to install

RIGHT, PRIMARILY FOR new construction, is a one-piece tub/shower that offers an optional cap to finish off walls and ceiling.

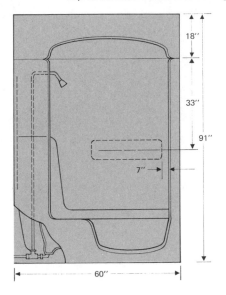

BELOW RIGHT, ideal for modernizing existing bathrooms, this unit will fit through doorways as narrow as 26 in. Strong, rigid and leakproof.

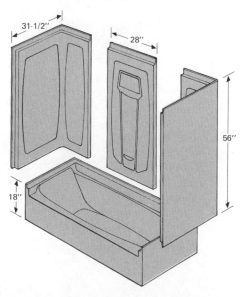

■ CERAMIC TILE surrounding a bathtub looks nice, but it presents two problems for homeowners: All those grout lines between the tile are hard to clean, and as the house settles, there's the periodic job of recaulking the crack that invariably develops where the tub and tile meet.

Happily, several makers of tub/showers have done something about it and are offering sectional and unitized bath units in reinforced fiberglass. Interlocking sections become a single leakproof assembly, making cleaning easier than ever before and ending crack filling for good.

From a remodeling and modernizing standpoint, these new no-tile tub/showers are made to order for the do-it-yourselfer. Being molded of lightweight but strong fiberglass, the tub and wall sections are easy for one person to

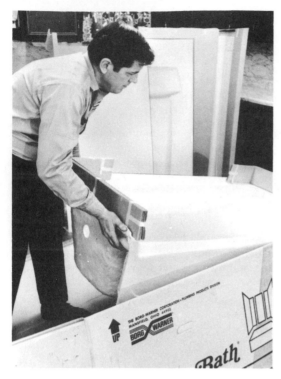

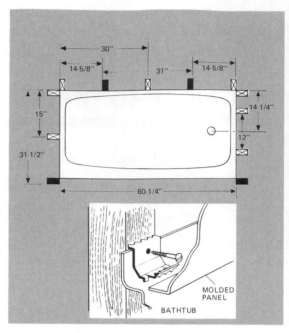

EXISTING FRAMING requires four additional studs (diagram) for attaching three panels in the system. Barbed fasteners lock the panel.

carry upstairs, through doorways and into place. They can be installed in any standard 5-ft. alcove in a matter of hours with little more than an electric drill, screwdriver and level.

The pictures here show how easily these pieces go into place. Once the alcove is stripped of the

old plasterboard and additional studs are added as required, installation is accomplished in four steps.

First step: The tub is set in place and leveled. A leveling runner on the bottom of the tub permits shimming if necessary. The tub is held with

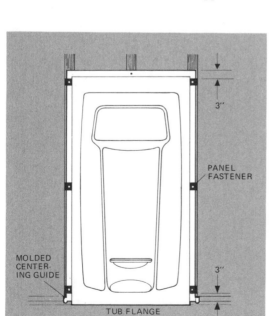

TWO GUIDES in the tub flange serve to position and align the center panels on the studs. Six panel fasteners, placed as shown, attach panels to studs.

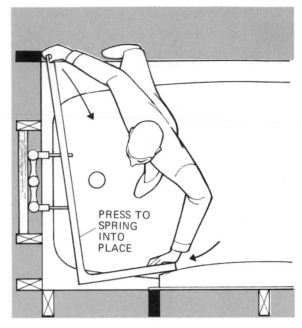

PRESS TO
SPRING
INTO
PLACE

TO INSTALL the L-shaped corner panel, place it in position as shown, spring it slightly to clear the edge of the center panel and let it snap back.

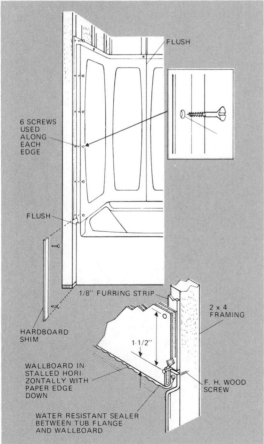

FLUSH

6 SCREWS
USED
ALONG
EACH
EDGE

FLUSH

1/8" FURRING STRIP

2 x 4
FRAMING

HARDBOARD
SHIM

1-1/2"

F. H. WOOD
SCREW

WALLBOARD IN-
STALLED HORI-
ZONTALLY WITH
PAPER EDGE
DOWN

WATER RESISTANT SEALER
BETWEEN TUB FLANGE
AND WALLBOARD

four special fasteners attached to studs with screws. Overflow and drain connections are made and tested.

Second step: The center wall panel is attached to the studs with fasteners and screws. Guides molded in the flange of the tub center the panel.

Third step: Holes for the faucets, spout and shower head are located and drilled through the corner panel with a hole saw.

Fourth step: Finally, the two L-shaped corner panels are inserted into fasteners along the center panel and pressed into place. Top and front edges of the panels are secured to the studs.

WATERTIGHT JOINTS are assured by caulking vertical and horizontal seams with mildew-resistant sealant. Surplus sealant can be removed with turpentine.

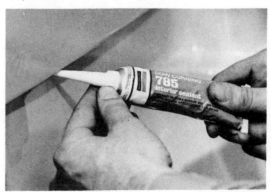

Create the illusion of a sunken tub

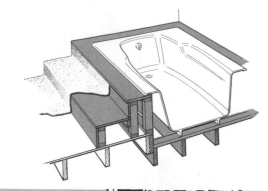

■ WHEN MODERNIZING a bathroom, you probably think you're limited to replacing old fixtures with new ones and possibly adding tile or carpeting. You're stuck with the original layout, and your new fixtures have to stay in the same old spots.

But when an adjoining room makes it possible to move a wall back a few feet, no longer are you

limited to a 5 x 7-ft. floor plan. With an enlarged area, you can start thinking ''sunken tub''—the latest innovation in modern bathroom planning.

A true sunken tub, of course, requires extensive structural modifications. A raised platform, however, can actually create the illusion of a sunken tub that's just as dramatic and attractive as a real one. The examples here show how a rim tub can be set in a wood-framed platform surrounded by steps and covered with shag carpet. In one (left), a 20-in.-high tub is in a well a little below floor level; in the other (above), a 14-in.-high apron tub sits on the floor and wood-slatted, split-level platforms are built around it.

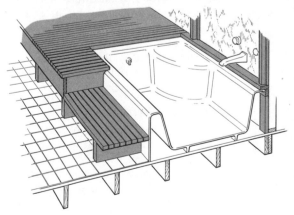

Victorian bathroom

■ YOUR GRANDMOTHER'S bathroom is popular again. Those white porcelain knobs, marble-topped sinks, funny toilets and tubs with claw feet are being reinstalled in new bathrooms all over the country. Unfortunately, most homes from that period have been replaced or remodeled, and over the years the "old" bathroom was one of the first rooms to go. But you can still have a Victorian bathroom in your home—a genuine one if you have time and diligence, or just a bathroom with a period feeling with the right furnishings.

First you must familiarize yourself with the objects and style of the Victorian home in general and the bathroom in particular. There are two places to start—the library and the local antique store. Current home and remodeling magazines frequently have articles and sometimes special issues devoted to Victoriana. Many books on turn-of-the-century architecture and furnishings have been reprinted because of the renewed popularity of this period. Study the photos or drawings and take note of the elements you might like to include in your proposed bathroom. In addition to fixtures and hardware, notice the other details. For example, several styles of curtains can give you a definite look, and you may want to install decorative moldings or even wainscoting. This half-paneled wall was common in the last century, and materials to do it are available in most lumberyards today.

Sources for fixtures

Once you have an idea of what to look for, many antique stores or curio shops may contain items that you can use for your project, even if it's just a soap dish, towel bar or old mirror. The ordinary "antique" store is your best bet; the fancy shop with expensive Colonial or imported antiques may not have anything you want, al-though its proprietors might be able to tell you where else to look. Somewhere you'll strike gold—the old porcelain toilet or antique bathroom sink. Only buy fixtures that are completely intact, without cracks or breaks. If the plumbing parts seem in good shape, you may be able to reuse them, but don't worry if these parts are missing or unusable. A large plumbing supply house can provide new parts or adaptors to make them work like new. Flea markets and tag sales are also good places to get usable fixtures. The porcelain will clean up easily with household detergent, and even stubborn stains will yield to an application of oxalic acid crystals from any drugstore. Old-style claw-foot bathtubs are widely available and should be inexpensive. Once you start looking for them, you'll bump into them everywhere. It's not uncommon to rescue one from a farmer's barn or water trough. Their cast-iron body is extremely durable and will last for another hundred years even if it's rusty on the outside. If you're lucky, the enamel inside will be usable with a good cleaning. If not, the tub can be resurfaced by a professional with a fresh enamel coating. Just remember that any cast-iron tub is very heavy; you'll need a pick-up truck or large station wagon to transport it and a few strong friends to help move it.

If you don't have time or the opportunity to find every fixture or part that is a genuine period item, don't despair. There are reproduction items on the market today for anything you might need. Home supply stores may have some of the things you want, or you can try mail-order houses.

Manufacturers have also noticed the new interest in older products. At least one major producer of bathroom fixtures is now offering an old-style toilet complete with brass and oak trim.

The illustrations shown here are from a real bathroom constructed in a new house. The owners wanted a Victorian bathroom; they began collecting fixtures, knobs and parts even before building began. From tag sales, curio shops and house salvage yards, cartons and boxes of this and that accumulated.

The bathroom actually began with the old cedar door with its ornate moldings and hardware. It was a $15 purchase at a garage sale and made a perfect door for a future bathroom. The tub, basin and toilet all have interesting histories.

The Victorian tub

Outside a plumbing supply store, the claw-foot tub was for sale. A deal was struck, including a new faucet. The enamel lining only needed cleaning. The rust and scale on the outside was prepared with a wire brush and then painted with a quality metal paint. As a treat to the grand old tub and the bathroom, the claw feet were sent to a plating shop to be bronzed. Because of its weight and bulk, the tub was hauled into the bathroom before the partition walls were erected. Standard drainpipe fittings and water supply shutoff valves were purchased at a home supply outlet. Connections were made by a plumber, using the same tools and materials as for any tub.

Not only is it a distinctive fixture of this Victorian bathroom, but it also provides a quality bath. It can be filled deep with water, and it's long enough for even the tallest adult to be comfortable while bathing.

The basin

The hundred-year-old marble-topped basin had been stored in a basement until it surfaced at a garage sale. It had only one hole for a faucet as it came from strictly cold-water days. Rather than bore another hole, a combined hot and cold single-hole faucet was fitted in the original place.

The toilet

Looking almost like a procelain rhinoceros, the stylish old toilet didn't cost this owner a thing except for new parts and fittings. It was discovered in a neighbor's yard, long discarded beneath some wild blackberry vines. An antique oak water tank to match was acquired in a trade for a restored chair. Installation involved only attaching the new connections, water and drain, just as you would with a new toilet.

The cost of this new yet old bathroom was less than buying everything fresh and new, but because of the care for details described it took much more time to plan and assemble. If you like the idea, look around your town—you may be surprised by what you find.

AN OLD-TIME BATHROOM with real Victorian fixtures, installed in a brand-new house.

Towel racks you can make

■ RATHER THAN PURCHASE towel racks for the bathroom, you can use the inexpensive towel bar designs shown. They are easy to make, and their blind construction and attachment give a clean, modern look.

Turn a 1⅜-in.-dia. bar on the lathe from glued-up 1½-in. stock. Dowels you can purchase will also work. Each bracket is made from two pieces of wood glued together with their grain directions at right angles for strength. Brackets and bars are stained and finished with two coats of urethane varnish, rubbed lightly with steel wool between coats.

The Early American towel rack shown is made of maple, with a Danish oil finish. You can also use white pine or walnut.

EARLY AMERICAN rack lets you swing towels against wall or into easy reach.

CANTILEVERED towel bar has places for toothbrush and drinking cup.

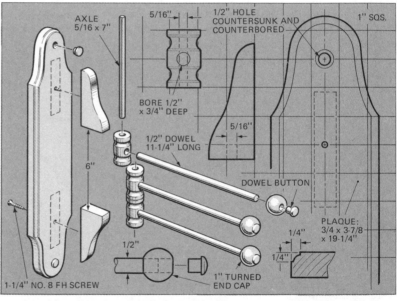

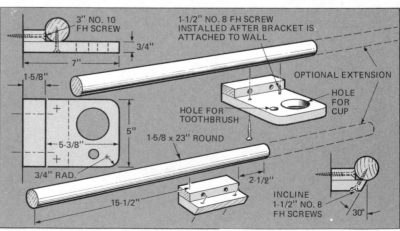

DOUBLE-ENDED version of towel bar omits brush and cup holder.

Early American shaving console

■ A CHARMING decorative piece for almost any room, this Early American shaving console is also functional. You can use it to hold shaving gear or other items. A shelf above the mirror can display an old shaving mug, and the small drawer provides more than adequate storage for the usual assortment of shaving paraphernalia. Additionally, a comb and brush box is located at the base, which is fitted with an American eagle hook that serves as a small towel holder.

Even if the console is not used for its original intended purpose, its colonial look fits in well in any room—including the kitchen where it can be hung next to the telephone to hold pads, pencils, calendars and other items.

The shaving console shown is built of cherry; if you prefer, it will still look good in walnut or knotty pine. If you wish, a side-view mirror salvaged from an old car can be used for the looking glass.

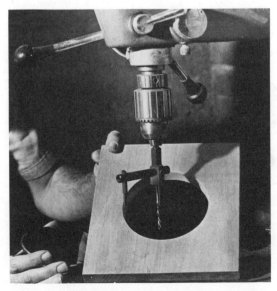

THE MIRROR CUTOUT in the rear panel is made with a circle cutter in a drill press or with a sabre saw.

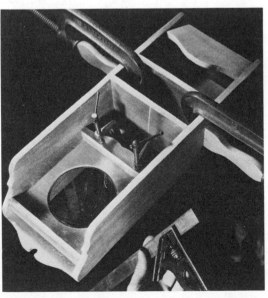

BRACKETS for candle holders are glued and clamped to the side panels. Drawer is last step.

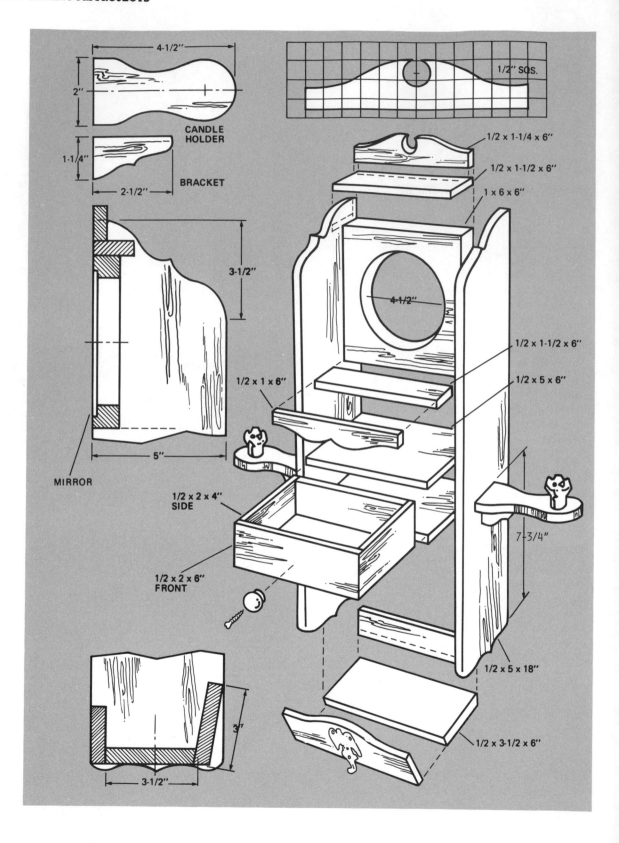

4-1/2"

2"

CANDLE
HOLDER

1-1/4"

BRACKET

2-1/2"

1/2" SQS.

1/2 x 1-1/4 x 6"

1/2 x 1-1/2 x 6"

1 x 6 x 6"

3-1/2"

4-1/2"

1/2 x 1-1/2 x 6"

1/2 x 5 x 6"

1/2 x 1 x 6"

5"

MIRROR

1/2 x 2 x 4"
SIDE

7-3/4"

1/2 x 2 x 6"
FRONT

1/2 x 5 x 18"

3"

3-1/2"

1/2 x 3-1/2 x 6"

Shaving cabinets you can make

■ GOT THE FEELING you're being gradually squeezed out of the medicine cabinet by teenagers and your better half? When there's hardly room left for you to use, it's time to move out and into one of these handsome shaving bars. Placed off limits to everyone else, they'll keep everything right at hand to give you that well-groomed look.

Both designs you see on these pages are wall mounted and have their own mirrors. Both feature counters, one a drop-front affair, the other an inside ledge. The former provides storage behind a lift-up mirror, the latter inside a swinging front. To top it off, both are smart looking and make handsome additions to any bathroom wall.

The bars combine select cabinet woods, with bright aluminum, glass and gleaming mosaic tile, and one of the handiest tools for putting all four together is a heat-type electric glue gun since it's made to order for bonding glass, tile and metal to wood. Using stick glue which bonds in 60 seconds, the gun eliminates the need for clamps.

The cabinet shown on this page is made of ½-in. solid walnut and fitted with a hardboard back. The ends are made right and left hand, and the closeup detail shows how they are grooved at the rear for the ⅛-in. back and at the front for the $^9/_{16}$-in. sliding mirror. The latter is glued to a plywood backing which is rabbeted top and bottom for aluminum-angle handles, and along the sides to fit the grooved ends. The mirror is cemented to the plywood with the glue gun.

HANDY DROP-FRONT COUNTER reveals additional storage behind it. Magnetic catch holds counter shut.

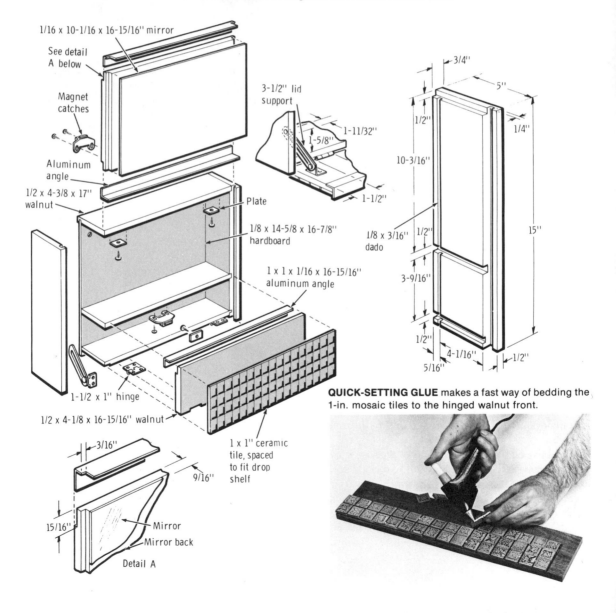

1/16 x 10-1/16 x 16-15/16" mirror

See detail A below

Magnet catches

Aluminum angle

1/2 x 4-3/8 x 17" walnut

Plate

3-1/2" lid support

1-11/32"

1-5/8"

1-1/2"

1/8 x 14-5/8 x 16-7/8" hardboard

1 x 1 x 1/16 x 16-15/16" aluminum angle

1-1/2 x 1" hinge

1/2 x 4-1/8 x 16-15/16" walnut

1 x 1" ceramic tile, spaced to fit drop shelf

3/4"

5"

1/2"

1/4"

10-3/16"

1/8 x 3/16" dado

1/2"

15"

3-9/16"

1/2"

4-1/16"

5/16"

1/2"

QUICK-SETTING GLUE makes a fast way of bedding the 1-in. mosaic tiles to the hinged walnut front.

3/16"

9/16"

15/16"

Mirror

Mirror back

Detail A

Since magnetic catches are used to hold the mirror in the raised position and are screwed to the plywood from the back, the mirror assembly must be in place before the ends of the cabinet are finally glued. Because of the catches, you can't slide the mirror in place from the top.

An aluminum angle across the top provides a handle for the tile-faced drop front. When gluing this, as well as the two metal strips to the mirror, the aluminum should first be heated so it's warm

when you apply the stick glue. A magnetic catch holds the drop front shut, and a desk-lid support holds it level when open.

The swing-front cabinet detailed on these two pages consists of two separate assemblies, one nesting inside the other. The three-sided box holding the mirror is made of ½-in. solid walnut and has a hardboard back. Note how the parts are grooved and rabbeted to accept a post to which the swinging front is hinged. Since the weight of the latter is on this post, metal corner braces are added for extra support.

Pine and hardboard are used for the front unit, the pine for the ends. Aluminum angle cemented to the three shelves provides retaining edges. The swinging front is completely painted in a three-color pattern, whereas the walnut members are stained and varnished.

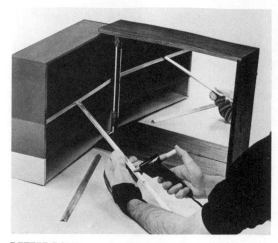

BETTER BOND is assured when cementing aluminum to the wood shelves if metal strip is first heated.

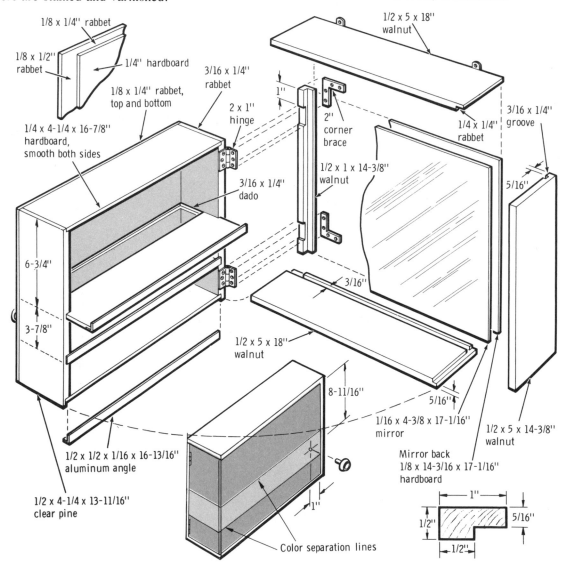

1/8 x 1/4" rabbet

1/8 x 1/2" rabbet

1/4" hardboard

1/8 x 1/4" rabbet, top and bottom

1/4 x 4-1/4 x 16-7/8" hardboard, smooth both sides

3/16 x 1/4" rabbet

2 x 1" hinge

3/16 x 1/4" dado

6-3/4"

3-7/8"

1/2 x 1/2 x 1/16 x 16-13/16" aluminum angle

1/2 x 4-1/4 x 13-11/16" clear pine

Color separation lines

1/2 x 5 x 18" walnut

1"

2" corner brace

1/2 x 1 x 14-3/8" walnut

3/16"

1/2 x 5 x 18" walnut

8-11/16"

1"

1/16 x 4-3/8 x 17-1/16" mirror

Mirror back 1/8 x 14-3/16 x 17-1/16" hardboard

3/16 x 1/4" groove

1/4 x 1/4" rabbet

5/16"

5/16"

1/2 x 5 x 14-3/8" walnut

1"

1/2"

1/2"

5/16"

1/2"

Guide to small batteries

■ THINK BACK. Not long ago you had no electronic games, LCD watches, cassette recorders, television games or portable fluorescent lights. Now you do. And they all gobble batteries, which are no longer cheap.

Luckily, 85 percent of batteries sold are 9-volt radio flat cells or AA, C and D round cells. It makes selection much easier; there are more than 400 different batteries available.

Carbon-zinc batteries

The common carbon-zinc dry cell has been sold for more than 90 years. Today, it is still the most widely used battery. Because of its low cost, in low-drain applications such as in radios, it can outperform the next best battery (the alkaline) by two to one in cost-per-hour use.

But—because of its internal chemistry—heavy, continuous current drain drives its efficiency way down. The faster you have to draw out power, the less you get. Other batteries have this problem, too, but not to the degree of the carbon-zinc.

Therefore, if you have a super-strong, walking, talking, motorized space robot that you want to show off to friends, avoid using carbon-zincs. The huge current appetite of this type of device will exhaust the batteries rapidly.

Despite this, there are some heavy-drain situations where it is smart to use a carbon-zinc. A flashlight or toy that draws heavy current may be used so infrequently that even a carbon-zinc won't run down. There is little point in buying a more expensive battery when its capacity will never be used.

Current drain isn't the only consideration. For example, carbon-zincs are essentially useless below 20° F. So forget using them for auto-winding your camera on a ski trip. However, their performance improves steadily with increased temperatures, reaching a peak at about 100° F.

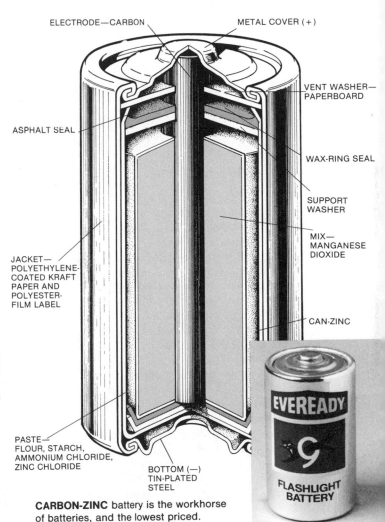

ELECTRODE—CARBON

METAL COVER (+)

VENT WASHER—PAPERBOARD

ASPHALT SEAL

WAX-RING SEAL

SUPPORT WASHER

MIX—MANGANESE DIOXIDE

JACKET—POLYETHYLENE-COATED KRAFT PAPER AND POLYESTER-FILM LABEL

CAN-ZINC

PASTE—FLOUR, STARCH, AMMONIUM CHLORIDE, ZINC CHLORIDE

BOTTOM (—) TIN-PLATED STEEL

CARBON-ZINC battery is the workhorse of batteries, and the lowest priced.

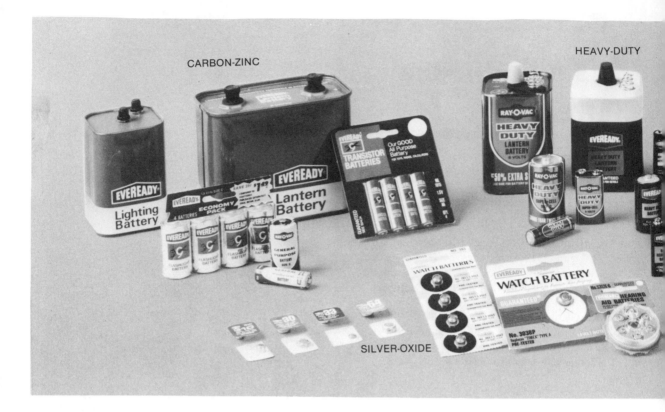

CARBON-ZINC

HEAVY-DUTY

SILVER-OXIDE

Important: Just because carbon-zinc batteries perform well in the heat, don't expect that they will store better that way.

High temperatures will greatly accelerate self-discharge, causing rapid battery deterioration and destroying their otherwise good shelf life.

You've probably seen batteries marked "heavy duty." But, are they really?

Generally, they are a form of carbon-zinc that uses a different construction and an electrolyte (zinc chloride).

You get 50 percent more capacity and somewhat better cold-temperature performance, along with—you guessed it—a 50 percent higher price tag.

You get what you pay for. Alkalines outperform all except the expensive, special types. They are good at high currents, work well in the cold, and have an excellent shelf life. In sum, they perform well in precisely the areas in which the carbin-zinc fails.

When the carbon-zincs are suffering under heavy currents, losing 90 percent of their capacity, it's the alkalines' turn to shine. Now they have the advantage, by a whopping 5 to 1 margin. What they say in the ads about alkalines is true. In toys, photoflash and other heavy-current devices, don't even consider another battery.

Of course, there has to be a break-even point. Generally, it falls at medium currents. However, since rest periods help carbon-zincs, the break-even point rises to somewhat higher currents with intermittent use. Also, the edge goes to the alkalines if you need very long (over five years) shelf life.

Alkalines and carbon-zincs share what is called a sloping voltage discharge. This means that their voltage falls gradually as they are discharged. The lower the cutoff your device can tolerate, the more energy you will get from the battery.

The major battery cards are on the table, and you've picked the best hand. So that's it; you're not going to save any more. Wrong! How would you like to take your low costs and cut them in half, or even two-thirds?

Just look for sales! Don't laugh. This one tip may save you more than anything we've said so far. The battery-marketing structure is such that there are often sizable discounts (and cash rebates) of 50 percent or more off list price.

Silver-oxide, the type of battery that powered the lunar buggy, would make a fantastic battery for your flashlight. It would power it three times as long as an alkaline, and your light wouldn't dim at all until the battery was totally exhausted.

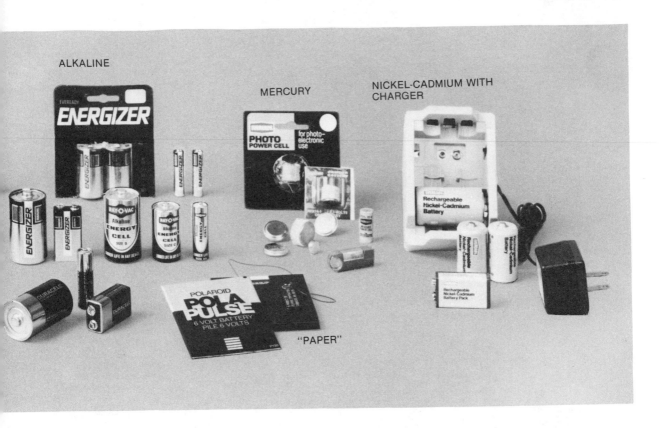

ALKALINE

MERCURY

NICKEL-CADMIUM WITH CHARGER

"PAPER"

There's just one tiny catch —it would cost $9.10 per hour!

Here on earth, you'll find silver-oxide batteries in watches, calculators, hearing aids and cameras as "button" cells. They are ideally suited to these applications because they have very high energy content for their size. Unlike carbon-zincs and alkalines, the voltage doesn't fall gradually during discharge, and this is important for the accuracy of watch circuits. Yet, despite their tiny size, they cost about $3 each.

Like the silver-oxide, mercury batteries find wide use in button-cell applications, but they cost half as much. However, *you can't indiscriminately replace a silver cell with a mercury.* This is because mercury has a lower operating voltage (1.35 or 1.4 volts). Many circuits, especially timekeeping ones like watches, can't take the one-fifth of a volt difference between the silver-oxide and mercury.

Luckily, hearing aids, which use up a lot of batteries, will not be damaged by a change from silver to mercury. Often, the only ill effect, if any, is slightly lower volume. In the future, we probably will see more devices designed around the cheaper mercury system.

Recently, alkaline button cells have appeared on the market as inexpensive replacements for the silver-oxide and mercury, which have a flat voltage discharge. The alkaline doesn't, and this can cause a problem in some devices, particularily watches.

If you find that your battery costs are high, then you need rechargeable nickel-cadmium (nicad) batteries. Once you get past the initial high cost, you have virtually free batteries for life, because they can be recharged over 1000 times. Often, the cost per discharge cycle is under a penny.

Usually, they come in the AA, C, D and 9-volt radio sizes. Unlike the button cells, you don't have to worry about the fact that the nicad has a 1.25 voltage rating. The devices that are designed to run on these batteries take into account that the voltage of carbon-zincs and alkalines falls in use. So the nicad's lower voltage is okay.

These batteries can crank out current levels that would put the powerful alkaline to shame. That's why you see them in extra-heavy-current applications, like hedge trimmers and soldering irons.

Recently, lead-acid lantern batteries appeared on the market. These are rechargeable, have a "gelled" electrolyte, and don't need added water. If you use over two lantern batteries a year, these batteries would be a good investment.

COMPARISON OF BATTERY LIFE

Type	Voltage	Composition	Weight (in ounces)	*Low drain	Hours of life	*Medium drain	Hours of life	*High drain	Hours of life	Approx. price
AAA	1.5	Carbon zinc	0.3	2	300	10	43	50	2.3	$ .35
AA	1.5	Carbon zinc	0.52	5	240	30	25	100	2.5	.35
C	1.5	Carbon zinc	1.5	10	220	50	20	250	1.5	.45
D	1.5	Carbon zinc	3.0	20	260	100	45	300	4.3	.45
9V	9.0	Carbon zinc	1.5	5	80	10	38	25	1.0	.99
AA	1.5	Zinc chloride	0.6	5	275	30	38	100	6.0	.50
C	1.5	Zinc chloride	1.6	10	330	50	56	250	7.0	.65
D	1.5	Zinc chloride	3.3	20	375	100	65	300	13.0	.65
9V	9.0	Zinc chloride	1.5	5	94	10	45	25	15.0	1.59
AAA	1.5	Alkaline	0.4	2	375	10	73	50	10.0	.90
AA	1.5	Alkaline	0.75	5	340	30	54	100	13.0	1.90
C	1.5	Alkaline	2.2	10	470	50	90	250	13.0	1.13
D	1.5	Alkaline	4.5	20	470	100	91	300	29.0	1.13
9V	9.0	Alkaline	1.6	10	52	30	17	60	8.0	2.25
A76	1.5	Alkaline	0.09	0.1	950	1	90	10	8.0	.99
AA	1.4	Mercury	1.05	5	480	30	80	100	23.0	1.90
675	1.4	Mercury	0.09	0.1	2200	1	215	5	42.0	3.25
AA	1.25	Nickel Cadmium	1.95	5	100	30	17	100	5.0	3.80
C-D	1.25	Nickel Cadmium	2.2	20	60	100	12	300	4.0	4.40
509	6.0	Carbon zinc	21.5	20	500	150	60	500	10.0	2.50
76	1.5	Silver	0.08	0.1	1900	1	190	5	37.0	2.40
544	6.0	Silver	0.5	0.1	1900	1	190	5	37.0	13.90
303	1.5	Silver	0.09	0.1	1650	1	165	5	32.0	4.15
357	1.5	Silver	0.08	0.1	1650	1	190	5	37.0	4.15

* Measured in milliamperes.
Note: 85 percent of carbon zinc and zinc chloride batteries, 95 percent of silver and mercury, 50 percent of nickel cadmium batteries get one year shelf life.

HOW DIFFERENT TYPES OF BATTERIES WORK

	Performance at:			Performance at:		Shelf life at:		
	Low current drain	Medium current drain	High current drain	Low room temp.	High room temp.	Low room temp.	Medium room temp.	High room temp.
Carbon-zinc	E	G	P	P	G	G-E	G	P
Zinc chloride	E	G-E	F-P	F	G	G-E	G	P
Alkaline	E	E	G	G	G	E	E	G-E
Nickel-cadmium	E	E	E	G	G	E	E	G-E
Mercury	E	E	F-E*	F	E	E	E	G
Silver oxide	E	E	F-E*	F	E	E	E	E
Lithium	E	G	P	E	G	E	E	E
Lead-acid	E	E	E	F	G	F	F	F-P

* Depending on type.   Legend: E = excellent; G = good; F = fair; P = poor.

THE INFORMATION on this page is valuable. The chart above, "How Different Types of Batteries Work," outlines the relative strengths of each battery-chemical.

Once you decide on the battery chemistry, get specific data from the top chart, "Comparison of Battery Life."

Finally, use the chart at the right and the top chart to calculate battery life.

You may see lithium cells taking over a good portion of the watch (button) and calculator market. They have an incredible shelf life that is measured in decades!

The "paper" battery shown in the photo is the same type of 6-volt, carbon-zinc battery that was an integral part of the Polaroid film packs. It is now available to the consumer as a separate battery for special applications where space is at a premium or there are momentary, large surges of current. Other than the fact that it's able to put out a 25-amp. pulse, it's similar in basic characteristics to the ordinary carbon-zinc battery of comparable size.

CURRENT DRAIN IN VARIOUS DEVICES
(Measured in milliamperes)

Device	Current Drain (volume)
Radios (with 9-v. battery)	9-12 (low) 10-15 (medium) 15-45 (high)
(with round batteries)	10-20 (low) 20-30 (medium) 30-100 (high) 100+ (blasting)
Cassette Recorders	70-130 (low) 90-150 (medium) 100-200 (high)
Calculators LED (9-v. battery)	20-30
LED (AA batteries)	40-100
Fluorescent (green)	20-50
LCD	under 1
Fluorescent Lamp (one 6-w. bulb)	500-1000
Flashlights	500-1000
Toys Motorized type Electronic games	400-2000 20-200
Video games	20-200
Cameras Photo flash Autowind	1000-2000 200-300
Watches LCDs LEDs	10-25; back-lighted 10-40, lighted
TVs (portable)	500-1500, depending on unit

Starting system troubleshooting guide

■ IT USUALLY HAPPENS when you're in a hurry. You've got a lot on your mind, maybe an important business meeting or a long-awaited social event. You move quickly to your car, slide in behind the wheel and turn the key. Nothing happens. The starter motor, that basic device, won't run.

The cranking circuit consists of these major components: the battery, battery cables and terminals, switch, neutral safety switch or clutch switch, solenoid switch or starter relay, cranking motor, the pinion and its drive, and the flywheel. The battery cables, starter and solenoid are wired together in a low-resistance circuit that carries large amounts of current. The key switch, neutral safety switch and solenoid switch are wired into a comparatively high-resistance circuit that carries much less current.

Most GM products and some Fords and Chryslers use a solenoid switch unit that is mounted on the outside of the starter motor. Other Fords have a relay switch somewhere in the engine compartment and an integral engagement mechanism within the starter motor. Most Chrysler starters have the solenoid built into the end of the starter motor.

If one of those components fails, you'll be left holding the key.

If absolutely nothing happens when you turn the key, there may be a problem in the high-resistance circuit that links the battery, key switch, neutral switch and solenoid switch. The battery may be completely dead or, in cases where the high-resistance circuit does not begin at the battery, there may be no voltage available at the point where it begins.

You can rule out a completely dead battery by simply switching on the lights. If the lights glow brightly, try starting the car again with them on. If they remain bright with the key in the start position, wiggle the gearshift selector or clutch pedal (on manual transmission cars) while you try again. If this makes the engine crank, the problem is a defective neutral safety switch or

THIS CHRYSLER CORP. cranking motor has a reduction gear that's set between the motor's armature shaft and the pinion gear shaft. This reduces the rotational speed at the pinion, but provides substantially increased cranking torque. The increased torque helps to eliminate hot-start problems on high-compression engines. The solenoid assembly is built into the end of the gear reduction starter. Consequently, the motor must be disassembled in order to repair the solenoid.

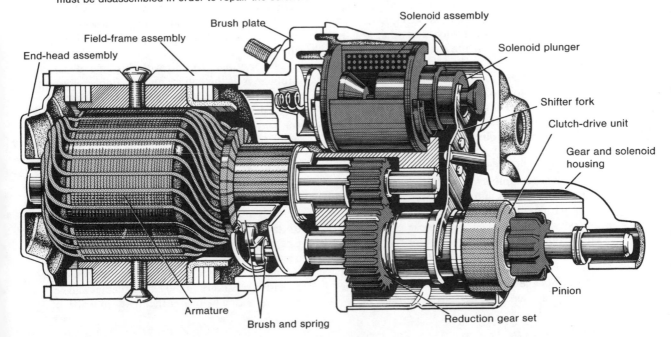

End-head assembly · Field-frame assembly · Brush plate · Solenoid assembly · Solenoid plunger · Shifter fork · Clutch-drive unit · Gear and solenoid housing · Pinion · Reduction gear set · Brush and spring · Armature

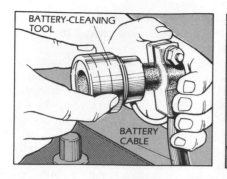

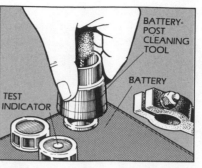

Many batteries have been replaced needlessly when a cleaning of terminals and posts would have solved the problem.

clutch switch. If wiggling doesn't help, use a test lamp or voltmeter to check for current at the neutral safety switch or the clutch start switch. In most cases, it will be found on the steering column, transmission or clutch pedal. Chrysler usually has a neutral relay mounted under the hood on the driver's side of the cowl. Connect the negative lead of your test instrument to a good ground and touch the positive lead to each side of the switch or relay with the car in **PARK** or with its clutch pedal depressed. Hold the key in the **START** position. Current should be available on both sides.

If current is available on only one side of the switch, it should be replaced. If current isn't available on either side of the switch, you probably have a defective key switch. If the dash indicators light with the switch in the **ON** position, you can rule out the last possibility.

If voltage is available on both sides of the neutral switch, check the terminal where the small wire of the high-resistance circuit is attached to the starter relay or solenoid switch. Most relays or solenoids will have two small wires. One is the trigger voltage from the switch. The other usually joins the coil to the starting circuit and provides a high-voltage charge to the ignition primary circuit to help start the car. With the key in the **START** position, voltage should be available at the terminal that is connected to the key switch circuit. If you're using a voltmeter, you should find more than 7 volts. If voltage is not reaching the solenoid or relay, there's a problem in the wire joining the safety switch and solenoid, or in the bulkhead connector where the underhood wiring loom plugs into the passenger compartment wiring.

You should also check for loose or corroded connections at the neutral switch or relay.

If voltage is available at the solenoid switch of a GM or Ford with starter-mounted solenoid, but the solenoid won't even click when the key is turned, the solenoid is defective and must be re-

placed. Most Chrysler products have a solenoid that is built into the starter motor. If this solenoid fails, the starter must be disassembled for repair or replaced with a new or rebuilt unit.

If you found voltage at the switch terminal of a Ford relay, check to see if a charge of at least 9.6 volts is available at the larger terminal of the relay with the key in the **START** position. If this is so, there is an open circuit between this point and the starter terminal or the starter is defective. If no voltage is available, replace the relay.

If you heard a good solid click when you first tried to start the car, try it again with the headlights on. If the headlights remain bright, the starter motor itself is probably defective, but the solenoid is okay.

If you heard a series of clicks, a weak click, or a click and a slow growling noise, try again with the lights on. If the lights go out completely or dim considerably, the battery may be dead, there may be excessive resistance in the circuit, the starter motor may be difficult to turn due to internal resistance, or the engine itself may be hard to turn due to internal damage. However, you can be certain that the principal problem is not in the switch circuit.

The best place to start with this type of starter problem is at the battery and its connections and cables. Check the battery for cracks or other obvious damage. Remove the terminals and check for corrosion or looseness. Replace any cables with terminals which have eroded or won't tighten. Don't replace the terminals. If your car is already equipped with replacement terminals (the kind that clamp the cable under a bolt-on strap), check the connection for corrosion. Even a little bit of corrosion at the point where the cable contacts the terminal can result in a no-start. Check the other end of the cables for proper connection also.

You can make a precise voltage-drop test for excessive resistance in the battery cables and connections with a voltmeter that reads in tenths of a

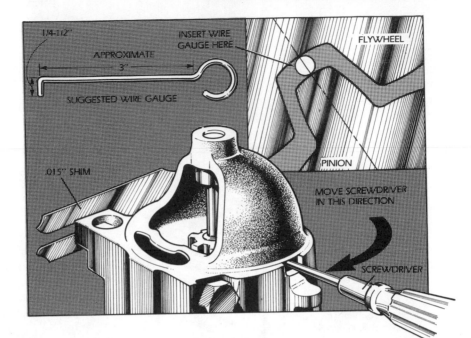

st pinion-to-flywheel clearance of
tarter, use a screwdriver to
nion into engagement with the
l. Then, using a .020-in. wire
measure clearance between pinion
nd flywheel as shown.

volt. Connect the positive lead of the voltmeter to the positive battery post and the negative lead to the starter. On starters with external solenoids, connect the negative lead to the large copper connector that joins the solenoid to the starter. On other starter motors, connect it to the terminal where the cable attaches. Attempt to crank the engine with the meter attached. The voltmeter should show less than ½ volt if the connections are good.

If a vehicle with an external solenoid fails this test, repeat the measurement, but this time attach the negative probe of the voltmeter to the terminal on the solenoid where the cable attaches. If there is less than ½ volt to this point with the engine cranking but there was more than ½ volt at the solenoid/starter connection, then the solenoid has excessive resistance and should be replaced.

To check ground-circuit resistance, connect the negative voltmeter lead to the negative battery post and the positive lead to the starter housing. Make sure it makes contact with the bare metal of the starter housing. With the key switch in the **START** position, the ground-circuit voltage drop should measure less than 0.2 volt.

If either ground or positive circuits fail the resistance test, clean and tighten connections and

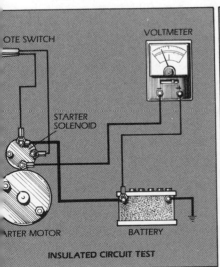

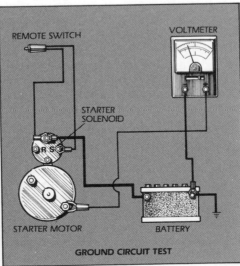

INSULATED CIRCUIT TEST

GROUND CIRCUIT TEST

TO TEST SYSTEM for too much resistance in the positive (insulated) circuit, connect the voltmeter's positive lead to the positive battery post, negative lead to the starter's positive terminal (far left). To check ground circuit resistance, connect the negative voltmeter lead to the negative battery post and the positive lead to the starter housing (left). Both are done by cranking the engine with meter attached. Meter should read less than ½ volt on the insulated circuit test, less than .02 v. on the ground circuit test.

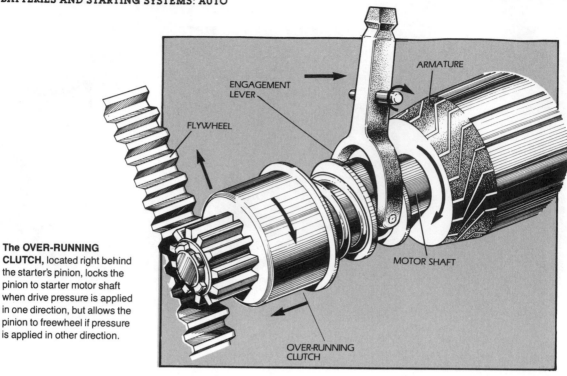

ENGAGEMENT LEVER

ARMATURE

FLYWHEEL

MOTOR SHAFT

OVER-RUNNING CLUTCH

The OVER-RUNNING CLUTCH, located right behind the starter's pinion, locks the pinion to starter motor shaft when drive pressure is applied in one direction, but allows the pinion to freewheel if pressure is applied in other direction.

repeat. If the problem persists, you can make the same measurements progressively closer to the battery until you find the problem area.

Once you've determined that the cables and connections are okay, check the battery's specific gravity.

Measure the battery's specific gravity following the instructions on the hydrometer. If it is low, charge the battery with a trickle charger. If the battery refuses to take a charge, it's no good.

Some of the recently produced maintenance-free batteries have built-in hydrometers that indicate state of charge by changing colors. Usually a green eye indicates a full charge, while a dark eye means that the battery is defective and should be replaced.

Once the battery is fully charged, connect the leads of a voltmeter to the positive and negative terminals of the battery. You should find roughly 12.5 to 14 volts. Turn the ignition to the **START** position. If voltage remains at or above 9.6 and the starter just clicks or turns slowly, the starter is defective. If the voltage drops below 9.6 either the starter is defective, the battery is defective or the engine is hard to turn.

That last cause is very unlikely, but you can check quickly by attempting to turn the engine by hand. Disconnect the negative terminal from the battery and try to turn the engine, using a

socket and breaker bar on the front hub bolt. Some engines can be cranked on the front hub of one of the accessories. If the engine turns with only medium difficulty (60 to 90 pounds break-away torque with a wrench), it's probably okay. If you have to pop sinews just to budge it, you had better check internal engine condition.

As for the other two causes, a defective battery or bad starter, you can attempt a common sense judgment call. If your battery took a charge, has no discolored electrolyte and is in good physical condition, the starter is most likely the problem. Attempting to jumpstart the car can help confirm this. If the battery is the cause of your problems, the jumpstart should make it crank faster. You might also turn on the lights, windshield wipers and heater motor and then attempt to blow the horn. If your battery can handle that much of a load, it is probably not the source of your difficulty.

If you have access to a volt/amp. meter with a built-in load device, you can test the battery capacity and compare it to specifications. This is the only way you can tell for sure that the battery is not at fault.

Most starter motors are equipped with an over-running clutch of some type. This device is right behind the pinion and prevents the starter from being spun and possibly damaged by the engine once it has started. It locks the pinion to the starter motor shaft when pressure is applied in one direction. The over-running clutch, in combination with the pinion and compression spring is sometimes called the starter drive or "Bendix."

If the over-running clutch fails to engage, the starter will spin, but it will not engage the engine. An over-running clutch that is on the verge of failure will engage briefly each time you attempt to start the car, but will soon disengage and free-wheel. Once the starter has been removed from the car, you can detect a faulty clutch by attempting to turn the pinion in both directions. It should turn freely in one direction, but not move at all in the other. The starter drive assembly can be replaced without replacing the rest of the starter, but the starter must be disassembled in order to do this.

Once you've determined that the starter is the source of your problem, remove the negative ground cable from the battery before attempting to remove the starter. Support the front of the car on jackstands. The rear wheels must be blocked, the emergency brake applied and the transmission in **PARK.** Determine how the starter can be maneuvered past other components before loosening the bolts.

Sometimes the wiring connections are easier to remove from above. On some applications with in-line engines, the starter is also removed from above. On GM applications, check for shims under the starter mount. These shims determine pinion-to-flywheel clearance. If there are any, they should be reinstalled with the new or rebuilt starter.

If you replace the starter motor on a GM car, you may have to adjust pinion-to-flywheel clearance. A sign of incorrect pinion clearance is a high-pitched whine during cranking or a high-pitched whine after the engine fires. To check pinion clearance, disconnect the negative battery cable, then insert a screwdriver in the small hole in the bottom of the starter's case at the pinion end. Use this screwdriver to push the starter pinion into engagement with the flywheel. Then, using a hooked wire gauge of 0.020-inch thickness, measure clearance between the peak of the pinion gear's tooth and the space between teeth on the flywheel gear. If clearance is less than 0.020, the starter should be shimmed away from the flywheel.

If the clearance is more than the specified 0.020 inch, check again with an 0.080-inch gauge. If clearance exceeds 0.080 inch, the starter should be shimmed toward the flywheel by installing a shim, on the outboard starter mounting pad.

Before you ever lay a wrench to a cranking system, remember that a great number of problems will produce the same type of poor cranking performance. Don't be too quick to condemn expensive parts. Make all appropriate measurements and evaluate them based on what you've observed.

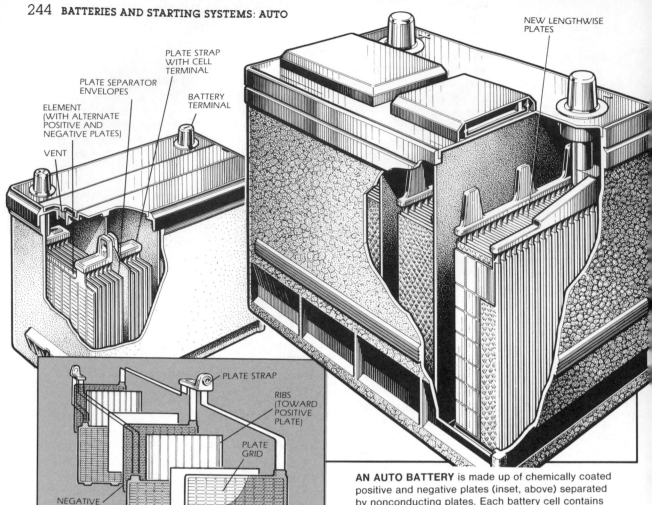

NEW LENGTHWISE PLATES

PLATE STRAP WITH CELL TERMINAL

PLATE SEPARATOR ENVELOPES

BATTERY TERMINAL

ELEMENT (WITH ALTERNATE POSITIVE AND NEGATIVE PLATES)

VENT

PLATE STRAP

RIBS (TOWARD POSITIVE PLATE)

PLATE GRID

NEGATIVE PLATE

POSITIVE PLATE

SEPARATOR

PLATE FEET

AN AUTO BATTERY is made up of chemically coated positive and negative plates (inset, above) separated by nonconducting plates. Each battery cell contains positive plates, negative plates and separators that are assembled into a unit called an element (small cutaway). Plate straps connect all the negative plates to the negative terminal, or post, while all the positive plates are connected to the positive post. In one new design (large cutaway), the short plates are mounted in each individual battery cell.

B attery care

■ OPINIONS DIFFER ON the most neglected part of a car. Some experts claim that the air cleaner is the most overlooked item, others say it's the sparkplugs. But AAA counts dead batteries as the culprit to win the no-start Oscar.

Keeping the battery of today's car in shape isn't difficult, providing the battery itself is capable of starting the car, and holding a charge.

It may seem foolish to check the battery to make sure it is the right one for the car. Just because the battery fits the carrier tray does not mean it is the right one. A battery must have the capacity, or amperes, needed to start an engine under all conditions in which the car might operate. The capacity of the battery is often tied to the guarantee that comes with it. Many makers offer a particular size battery with a three-, four- or five-year warranty.

The difference between them could be nothing more than the size or number of plates in the battery case. It is the plate surface area, working with the electrolyte, or acid, that determines the capacity of the battery.

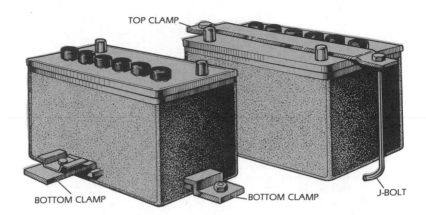

HOLD-DOWN clamps prevent the battery from bouncing around, which can cause internal damage. Bottom clamps require a special ridge around the bottom of the battery case.

TOP CLAMP

BOTTOM CLAMP

BOTTOM CLAMP

J-BOLT

How it works

Consider the battery for what it is—a lead-acid chemical reactor. It does not store electricity, nor does it manufacture electricity.

When we turn the ignition switch, a chemical reaction takes place in the battery. This chemical reaction will continue until most of the active material in the battery has been changed into lead sulfate. At this point, the positive and negative plates become chemically similar, and the chemical reaction grinds to a halt. In other words, the battery is dead.

This discharge reaction can be reversed by delivering a current to the battery, thus restoring the chemicals to their original form. The car's charging system, which includes the alternator, is responsible for providing the recharge current while the engine is running.

The capacity of the battery, or the amount of current (amperes) that it can produce without recharging, is determined by the amount of plate surface exposed to chemical action. The battery will lose plate area if the plates are not completely immersed in the acid solution. The plates of a battery will eventually become sulfated and inoperative even with normal care, but overcharging or allowing the battery to become fully discharged will speed up the sulfation of the plates.

Check battery mounts

Two of the major enemies of a battery are vibration and physical shock. When a battery is bolted in place it rides with the car and is somewhat protected by the car's suspension. But when the battery hold-down bracket is left off or has corroded away, the battery will bounce all over and is likely to sustain internal damage.

If the hold-down bracket is missing, you can probably get the necessary bolts and bracket at an auto parts store. If the parts store doesn't have a bracket that fits your car, you can buy the original equipment piece from the franchised dealer.

Some cars use a bracket that hooks into a ridge low on the side of the battery case. It is a small metal plate that's attached to the car by a bolt that threads into a cage nut on the inner fender well or battery carrier. Some replacement batteries on the market do not have the necessary ridge around the bottom of the case. On some cars equipped with this type of hold-down, the bolt may become corroded. When you attempt to remove it, it will often break. You cannot reuse this type of hold-down without removing the battery carrier, extracting the broken bolt or cage nut, and installing a new cage nut.

A 6- TO 10-AMP. trickle charger can recharge most batteries overnight. Fully discharged maintenance-free batteries require fast charging.

BATTERY CHARGER

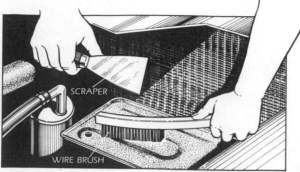

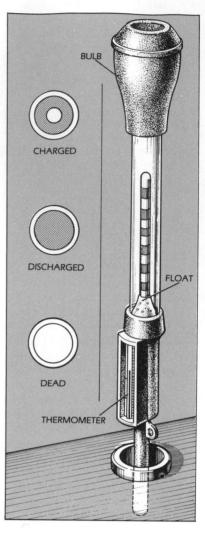

TO CLEAN a corroded battery tray (left), use a scraper and a wire brush to remove all corrosion, then spray with epoxy paint. Professional hydrometer gives most accurate indication of battery condition (right). Each cell should read 1.250. Some maintenance-free batteries contain a built-in "eye" to indicate battery condition accurately.

INEXPENSIVE VOLTMETER can be used to perform several battery tests. Attach the red voltmeter lead to the positive battery terminal and black lead to the negative.

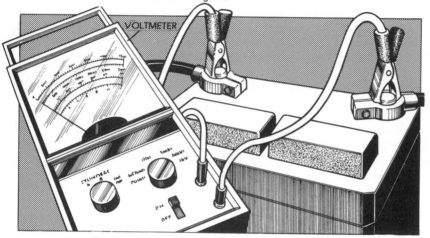

If you want to repair broken hold-down bolts, remove the battery and drill a couple of ⅜-in. holes at either end of the battery carrier. Don't attempt to drill the holes with the battery in place. It's easier to get at the carrier when the battery is removed and, more importantly, it's dangerous to operate electrical equipment near the battery. There is hydrogen gas present around the top of all batteries. Any spark could cause the battery to explode, splashing battery acid all over you, your clothes and your eyes. For this reason, you should always wear safety goggles when working around the battery.

Removing cables

There is a right and a wrong way to remove battery cables from the battery before servicing. The grounded battery cable, almost always the negative cable, should be removed from the battery first. If you slip and touch a part of the car's body with your wrench, there will not be any spark. However, touching a wrench from the live terminal, usually the positive post, to the car's body will create a dead short plus lots of sparks and heat. At the very least, this will cause the wrench to get hot and burn your hand.

Loosen the bolts on the battery clamps and use a battery clamp puller to ease the clamps off the posts. Now, with the holes drilled, snake a couple of universal-type J-bolts of the correct length into the holes. Stand the bolts up and return the battery to the carrier, then install a universal hold-down bracket across the top of the battery, between the J bolts.

If the battery tray itself is loose, it must be secured. Sometimes a bit of metal fabrication is needed, sometimes just a simple replacement.

Watch for corrosion

A battery that has been allowed to float loose in the battery tray will often leak acid that can eat away the inner fender panel, as well as the tray. It's wise to check the fender panel and all of the parts to which the tray mounts for damage. All of the surrounding metal should be cleaned thoroughly with a brush and a baking soda solution, rinsed with plenty of clear water, dried, and painted. The epoxy paint that is used on white spoked wheels gives excellent results.

The battery needs a supply of current to reverse the chemical action that causes discharge. At the same time, the car needs current for the ignition and accessories while it's running. The charging system provides enough for both. If the charging system is not working properly, the battery will discharge excessively, the plates will become sulfated, and the battery will wear out long before its time.

Charging system check

The place to start in charging system service is with a check of the alternator drive belt. It should be tight and have about ½ in. of play when you push on it with your thumb at a point halfway along its longest span. Twist the belt over and check it for cracking, glazing or fraying. Any damaged belt should be replaced. A glazed belt may appear to be okay, but it will slip, even when tight.

The charging system can be easily tested for general operation with a voltmeter. Set the meter on the 20-v. scale and attach the red lead to the positive battery terminal and the black lead to the negative battery terminal. With all accessories off, the engine warmed up and running at about 1,500 rpm, the voltmeter should read somewhere between 13.8 v.d.c. and 15.3 v.d.c. Any voltage less than 13.8 means the charging system needs work.

This test, of course, tells you only that the charging system is functioning. Considerably more elaborate testing is required to pinpoint charging problems.

Checking battery charge

You can test the battery for state of charge and capacity with a couple of simple tools. The first one—used on batteries that have removable caps—is a hydrometer. There are many types.

The float type uses a weighted float with numbers inscribed on the barrel. Draw just enough electrolyte up into the tube to raise the float, and read the specific gravity where the fluid level crosses the barrel. A battery fully charged and in good condition will read between 1.250 and 1.300. Each cell should be within .050 points of every other cell. A difference of over .050 indicates that the cell could be sulfated and the battery should be replaced, not recharged. If all cells are even, but well below the 1.250 mark, the battery should be recharged and retested until the hydrometer test gives a 1.250 reading.

The least expensive hydrometer uses five different balls in a glass tube. Each ball is of a different color and weight. As the concentration of acid increases, more balls will float until all of them are floating. This indicates a fully charged battery.

To test the battery, draw fluid from each cell in turn and record the number of balls floating. Return the fluid to its cell and test the next one. Each cell should float the same number of balls. If they don't, you can suspect that the cell with the lower number is defective or sulfated.

If all the cells read low (float only a few balls), then the battery should be recharged. A slow charger can be used and the charging should continue until all of the balls in the hydrometer float (or, until the reading is at least 1.250).

Some maintenance-free batteries have a built-in hydrometer. On many of these, you'll find a little window on top of the battery. Usually, a dark or black "eye" means that the battery is in need of recharge. A green eye means that the battery is at least 75 percent charged. A clear or yellow indicator means that the battery is defective and must be discarded.

There are many battery chargers on the market. For the average home shop a simple trickle charger with a 6- to 10-amp. charging rate will suffice. This charger will bring conventional batteries to full charge, but it may take several hours or overnight to do so.

A slightly discharged maintenance-free battery can often be brought to full charge on a small charger, but a fully-discharged battery of this type must be charged at very high current levels on professional equipment.

Checking battery condition

Your voltmeter can also be used to check the battery capacity and condition. With the voltmeter still connected to the battery's posts, disable the ignition by removing the coil cable from the distributor cap. Ground the cable to the block with a jumper wire to prevent arcing of the high-voltage spark that could cause a fire, shock you, or damage the ignition system. (On GM cars with HEI ignition, simply disconnect the small lead

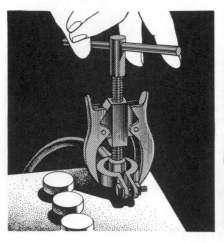

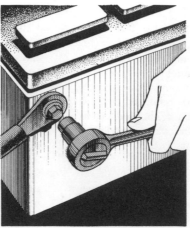

The easiest way to remove battery cable from a top-post battery is with an inexpensive cable clamp puller (left). Loosen the clamp bolt, then use the puller to lift clamp. On side-terminal batteries (right) you merely have to remove the terminal bolt.

connected to the BAT terminal on the distributor.)

With the ignition disabled as described above, engage the starter for 15 seconds. Let the system rest for 30 seconds and repeat the test for 15. This time, at the end of the 15 seconds, with the engine still cranking, read the voltmeter and record the reading. If the reading is above 10 volts for a maintenance-free battery—or above 9.6 volts for a conventional battery—the battery and starter are both good.

A low reading will not distinguish between a bad battery and a bad starter. If other conditions lead you to suspect that the battery has lost capacity, you can generally assume that it has.

Cleaning and reinstalling

To clean and maintain your battery, you will need a wire brush, a clamp and post cleaner, a box of baking soda, a paint brush, some water and a jar of petroleum jelly. Remove the cables. Mix some baking soda in a container with water to the consistency of wallpaper paste. Use the paintbrush to apply the paste to the top, sides and around the carrier of the battery. When it stops bubbling, flush with clear water. Coat the cable clamps, or terminals, with the mixture, as well. Then flush them with water—plenty of water.

Next, use the post and clamp cleaner to make the posts and inner clamp surfaces bright and shining clean. If the bolts on the clamps are eaten up by acid, replace them. If the clamps fit the posts too loosely, you can use a hacksaw to cut the slot in the clamps wider. This will allow the bolt to pull the clamp shut around the post. If the cable ends are too far gone to give a good connection, replace the complete cable.

Install the cable clamps, (positive first, then negative) and tighten each nut and bolt. Care

must be taken here. Installing the battery in the reverse polarity will damage the diodes in the alternator, the wiring harness and any electronic or computer equipment on the car. Once the cable clamps are on tight, a light coating of petroleum jelly will prevent corrosion.

Battery maintenance might seem like a lot of work, but getting reliable starts will make the effort worthwhile.

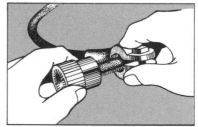

CLEAN THE BATTERY POSTS and cable clamps (above) with a special wire brush until they are shiny. You should use a battery carrier (below) or strap to lift heavy battery, lessening chance of damage or injury.

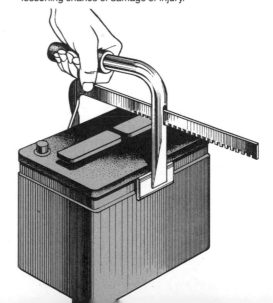

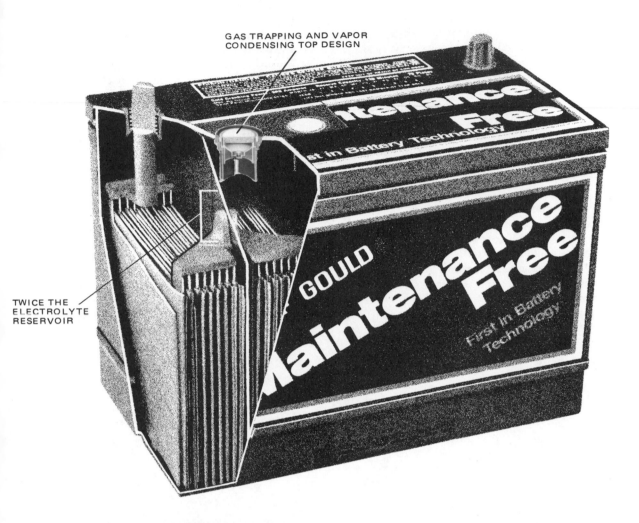

GAS TRAPPING AND VAPOR
CONDENSING TOP DESIGN

TWICE THE
ELECTROLYTE
RESERVOIR

Maintenance-free battery care

■ IN RECENT YEARS many of the major automakers have begun putting maintenance-free or low-maintenance batteries into their new cars. These also have become large sellers at retail stores, chain stores and oil companies. As such batteries become more popular, you should know how to maintain, test and recharge them.

What is 'maintenance-free'?

Some batteries called "maintenance-free" by store personnel or instore advertising are really low-maintenance types. Major battery manufacturers spell out, by labeling on the battery or in literature accompanying it, if the unit is truly maintenance-free.

Maintenance-free batteries are more expensive than low-maintenance batteries. Both cost more than conventional batteries, but cost is not the only difference. Whether a battery is low-maintenance, maintenance-free or conventional depends on its grid construction.

Battery grids are lattice networks that hold pastes of active materials, which form the positive and negative plates. Grids also conduct electric current from the plates to the poles.

In a conventional battery, grids are an alloy containing 5 to 6 percent antimony and the rest lead. In a low-maintenance battery, grids are an alloy of 2 to 3½ percent antimony. In a maintenance-free battery, antimony has been eliminated and replaced by a calcium-lead alloy.

The degree of maintenance a battery requires depends on the amount of its antimony content. By "maintenance" we mean how often it is necessary to check cells for water loss and clean battery terminals, cable connectors and battery case.

Antimony causes a battery to accept current after the battery is fully charged. This overcharging leads to a loss of water (electrolyte) because excessive current reacts on water, turning it into hydrogen and oxygen.

Electrolyte loss presents you with three maintenance tasks. First, you have to replenish the water.

Second, gases given off through battery vents settle on connectors and terminals, causing corrosion that can impede the flow of current to the starter motor. If corrosion is not cleaned off, the engine could fail to start.

Third, gases escaping from vents can settle on the battery case and create a self-discharging path, draining battery strength. This will require you to have the battery charged frequently if you don't wash it to eliminate the electrolytic salts. Electrolyte is an electrical conductor. Calcium-lead batteries—that is, maintenance-free—do away with these tasks.

Calcium-lead batteries just about turn themselves off when they become fully charged. They accept little more current. Therefore, in a calcium-lead battery, the gases emitted when overcharging takes place are reduced 90 to 97 percent. Water loss is kept to a minimum during a battery's lifetime.

In a vehicle with the voltage regulator set to limit voltage to 14.2 volts, it's possible for a battery with 5 percent antimony to accept up to 6 amps. in overcharge current. A calcium-lead battery will accept an overcharge current of less than 0.1 amp.

Two venting systems

Make no mistake about one thing: Every battery gives off gases. Calcium-lead and low-antimony batteries are no exceptions. Although

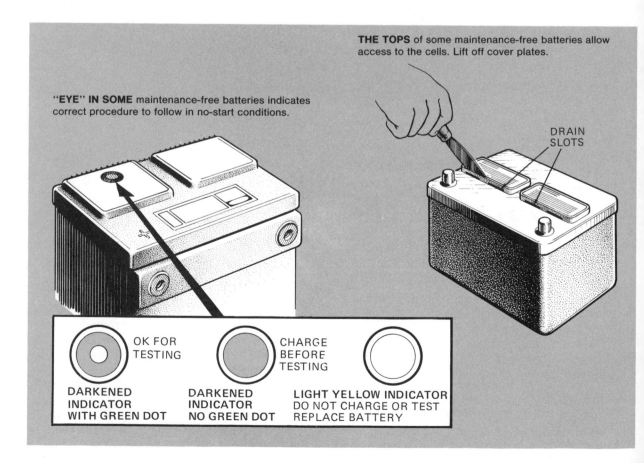

"EYE" IN SOME maintenance-free batteries indicates correct procedure to follow in no-start conditions.

THE TOPS of some maintenance-free batteries allow access to the cells. Lift off cover plates.

DRAIN SLOTS

OK FOR TESTING

CHARGE BEFORE TESTING

DARKENED INDICATOR WITH GREEN DOT

DARKENED INDICATOR NO GREEN DOT

LIGHT YELLOW INDICATOR DO NOT CHARGE OR TEST REPLACE BATTERY

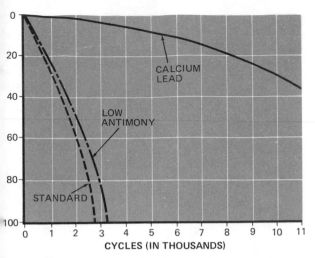

GRAPH SHOWS slight water loss of maintenance-free batteries using calcium-lead.

many maintenance-free batteries look sealed (the familiar vent caps are not present), venting must be built into the battery in some way. A battery that isn't vented has no way to purge itself of gases that accumulate inside and can cause the battery to burst.

Two methods of venting a maintenance-free battery are used—through tiny holes in the sides or ends of the battery, or through a microporous disc. Either method permits flame-retardant venting; that is, it prevents flames created externally from traveling into the cell and igniting explosive gases.

Installing a new battery

Installing a battery correctly is necessary to prevent damage, so let's run down the procedure.

When you buy a new battery you never know how long it's been in storage. Maintenance-free batteries have excellent shelf-life characteristics because of their low rate of self-discharge. They can remain in storage for at least 12 months without need for charging. However, you have no guarantee that a battery wasn't neglected. It may have been in stock long enough to lose charge. A booster charge of 20 amps. for two hours assures you that the battery will enter service fully charged. Charging is also advisable if the battery is being installed in cold weather or has been stored in a cold place.

Important: Do not charge a Delco Freedom battery if the visual indicator reveals a green dot.

Removing an old battery

As the battery is charging, remove the old bat-tery from the car, noticing the position of positive and negative terminals. To avoid accidental damage that the cross-switching of terminals and cable connectors may cause, mark pieces of masking tape (−) and (+) and place each on its respective cable: (−) on the ground cable (the one with one end connected to the engine block); (+) on the positive cable (the one that goes to the starter switch or starter relay).

Caution: Whenever you disconnect a battery, remove the ground (−) cable first. This minimizes the possibility of sparks shooting off that could ignite the hydrogen given off by a battery.

Inspect cables. If they are cracked, frayed or worn through, replace them. If cables are not worn, clean the connectors with a battery-cleaning tool or a wire brush. This may be the last time you will have to use a battery-cleaning tool. The small amount of gas given off by a maintenance-free battery is directed away from terminals and connectors, virtually eliminating corrosion.

Next, clean the battery hold-down and tray with a wire brush. Wash them with a weak solution of baking soda and water. Rinse and dry.

Place the new battery on the tray. See that its terminals line up with the correct battery connectors. *Connect positive cable first.*

Very important: Do not overtighten cable connectors. Doing so may distort the battery and cause early failure. Use a torque wrench. If the battery has side terminals, tighten bolts to between 60 and 90 in.-lb. or 6 ft.-lb. If the battery has posts extending from the top of the case, tighten the cable connectors to 15 ft.-lb.

Servicing a battery

A *low*-maintenance battery requires the same maintenance you've been giving conventional batteries, although not as often. This entails checking the electrolyte level every 12 months or 10,000-15,000 miles, keeping the battery and connectors clean, and testing the state of charge when a starting problem appears to be caused by battery failure.

Maintenance-free batteries require service when a starting problem occurs. This is why Delco-Remy equips its Freedom battery with an "eye." Some think that the "eye" reveals whether the battery is good or bad, but this is *not* the case. The "eye," or visual indicator, indicates the level and specific gravity of the electrolyte in *one* cell.

You don't have access to the cells of the Freedom battery to check electrolyte level or test electrolyte specific gravity. This battery is sealed. In normal vehicle operation, there is no need to view the "eye" until a starting complaint is involved. Then the "eye" reveals what procedure to follow.

If the "eye" has a green dot, it is safe to load-test the battery to determine if it is causing the starting problem. The amount of load placed on the battery depends on the model. The minimum voltage depends on temperature.

If minimum voltage is not attained during the load test (9.6 volts at 70° F. or above), replace the battery. The fact that the "eye" shows a green dot makes no difference. Remember: The "eye" doesn't tell if the battery is good or bad. If the "eye" is dark (no green dot), the battery should be charged before it is load-tested. Rate of charge varies with battery model and is outlined in service literature.

Caution: Charging should be halted when the green dot appears in the "eye" or when the maximum charge is reached, according to service instructions. If the "eye" is pale or light, do not charge or test the battery. The electrolyte has been depleted. Since water cannot be added, this is one situation that calls for replacing the battery.

Cells are accessible

If your maintenance-free battery does not have an "eye," you have access to cells, although it may not seem that way.

Some companies make no attempt to hide cell openings. For example, the Red Camel maintenance-free battery, manufactured by ESB, has conventional battery caps. The caps can be removed, allowing water to be added if a voltage regulator goes bad and excess current is permitted to reach the battery. Excessive current increases gassing and will cause premature battery failure if water is not replenished.

The Roughneck and Liberator batteries, manufactured by Prestolite, are two types of maintenance-free batteries that have cells hidden, but accessible. With the Liberator, the center cover is removed by pulling straight up on the ends. After checking electrolyte level, the cover is placed in position and pressed down firmly until it seats.

With a Roughneck battery, a knife is used to cut through the top plaque center section. Removing the plaque reveals individual screw-type vent plugs.

Hold onto your battery hydrometer if you switch to a maintenance-free battery that allows access to the cells. You can check the battery's state of charge in the usual manner.

If you are hesitant about cutting through the battery to get at cells, there is another way to determine state of charge besides using a hydrometer. Ford suggests the following steps:
● Perform a battery capacity test.
● Wait one minute.
● Measure *no-load* battery voltage. If it is 12.4 volts or better, the battery is adequately charged. If no-load voltage is less than 12.4 volts, a booster charge should be applied.

Battery Tips
● Avoid tipping a battery, even a maintenance-free battery. It's possible that electrolyte could leak out of the vents.
● The number one problem associated with discharged batteries is a loose generator drive belt.
● The charge voltage of maintenance-free batteries is more critical than with conventional batteries. A voltage regulator out of specification will result in a discharged battery if the setting is low, or premature water consumption if the setting is too high.
● If you are going to store a maintenance-free battery, keep it upright in a cool, dry place. Avoid a place where the temperature will be above 80° F. High temperature increases the rate of self-discharge. To prevent freezing, do not store the battery where the temperature goes below 32° F.
● You can jump-start a maintenance-free battery in the usual manner. However, cover the battery's top and/or ends with a clean cloth to block vent holes. This will prevent gas that may escape from possibly being ignited by a spark.

Don't electrocute your car battery

■ THE AMMETER supplies more useful information at a glance than any other instrument in your car. Unfortunately, the ammeter is not used much any more.

You are driving blind when you rely solely on warning lights. If you really want to know what's going on, build the auto electrical-system tester. This simple meter plugs into your car's cigaret lighter and supplies all the information of an ammeter and some extra.

An auto battery isn't just a black box that puts out exactly 12 volts until it dies. During normal car operation, it may vary from 12 to 15 volts depending on whether it is being charged or discharged. Hidden in small voltage shifts is plenty of information about the electrical system. A single volt can be the difference between a car that is running or one stuck somewhere with a dead battery.

Let's change the scale on a meter to spread the range of 12 to 15 volts over its face. Use a meter that normally reads 0 to 1 milliamp. to display the automobile's voltage.

Our electronic trick is to get the meter to display a voltage range between 12 and 15. To make our magic, we'll use a *zener diode* that will not conduct any electric current until there is a certain voltage across its leads. Our expanded meter will not indicate until voltage reaches 12. Then it reads correctly from 12 to 16 volts.

You'll also need a cigaret-lighter plug and a 3900-ohm resistor. Wire the diodes so that their polarity bands face this resistor, not the meter.

In a properly working car, before the car is started, with everything turned off, the meter reads about 12.5 volts. Open a car door and the meter will drop a notch due to the current drain of the dome light. The meter falls below 12 when the engine is cranked due to the tremendous current drain of the starter. The battery can fall as low as 9 volts. Remember, our meter scale starts at 12 volts.

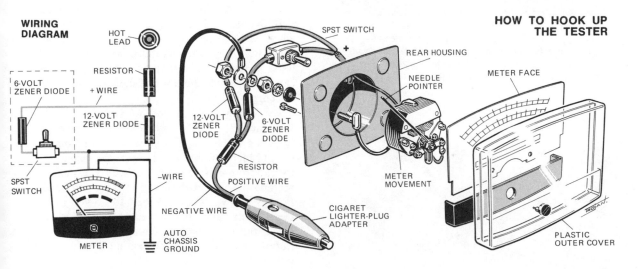

WIRING DIAGRAM

HOW TO HOOK UP THE TESTER

HOT LEAD — RESISTOR — + WIRE — 6-VOLT ZENER DIODE — 12-VOLT ZENER DIODE — SPST SWITCH — METER — −WIRE — AUTO CHASSIS GROUND — 12-VOLT ZENER DIODE — 6-VOLT ZENER DIODE — RESISTOR — POSITIVE WIRE — NEGATIVE WIRE — CIGARET LIGHTER-PLUG ADAPTER — SPST SWITCH — REAR HOUSING — NEEDLE POINTER — METER MOVEMENT — METER FACE — PLASTIC OUTER COVER

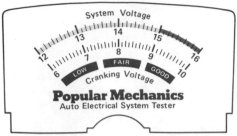

CUSTOMIZE your tester. Pop the clear cover from a Radio Shack 0-1 milliamp. No. 22-052 meter. Paste on the exact-size replacement face (above). Don't bend the pointer needle.

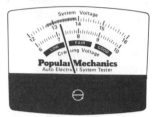

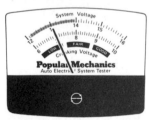

TEST READINGS: 12-12.8 (top left) normal vols with no use of battery; 12.8-13.8 (top right) undercharging, fast idle; 15.1-16 (middle left) overcharging, fast idle; 12-12.6 (middle right) engine off but lights on; 12.1-13.9 (bottom left) generator car at idle; 13-15 (bottom right) alternator car at idle.

A ONE-PIECE plug-in version is made by taping or gluing the lighter plug to back of smaller meter.

Once the car is started, the generating system supplies its electrical needs. System voltage is brought up to 14 to 15 volts.

Dead Meter

If the meter is below 12.8 and doesn't move in response to changes in engine speed, don't sit there and watch the needle fall. Get the car off the road immediately. But don't shut off the engine yet. Check to see if your fan belt is broken. If so, stop the engine right away.

If you have an intact fan belt, the charging system is dead and the battery is powering the electrical devices in the car. The coil is the first thing to die as the battery runs down. Don't waste time. Turn off all electrical accessories and head for the nearest service station.

If heavy electrical use makes the meter drop below 14 to 15 when the engine is going faster than idle, watch out. In severe cases, the meter never reaches 14 or 15 volts.

As the generator or alternator is called on to deliver more power, it drags harder on the fan belt. A loose belt slips, reducing output and system voltage. Tighten the fan belt.

If the meter stays near or above 15 during driving, the voltage regulator is set above the proper 14.6 volts. As you drive, the battery is being overcharged. Your dashboard light or original-equipment ammeter will not indicate there is a problem. They respond only to current, not voltage levels. The life of the battery is being shortened. Adjust or replace the regulator.

The meter never moving above 13.8 volts is the opposite of frying your battery. The regulator is set too low. The battery never gets a full charge. Your light or ammeter won't tip you off to this one either. Another symptom is weak cranking.

If, over several months, the meter falls farther when you turn on your lights than it did before, the battery is getting old and weak. Other symptoms include lazy cranking and, on generator cars, a noticeable dimming of the lights when the car engine is idling.

By adding a switch and a 6-volt zener diode, you can tell when you are not getting proper cranking voltage to start your car. Switching the 6-volt zener into the circuit lowers the meter scale to read from 6 to 9.5 volts. The scale is expanded, reading 6 volts on the left and 9.5 volts on the right. When you switch in the 6 to 9.5 volt range, the 12-volt zener has no effect in the circuit. Check out your cranking voltage by reading low, fair or good on the replacement meter face we've provided.

INDEX · VOLUME 2

SHOP GUIDE

CUSTOMARY TO METRIC (CONVERSION) Conversion factors can be carried so far they become impractical. In cases below where an entry is exact it is followed by an asterisk (*). Where considerable rounding off has taken place, the entry is followed by a + or a − sign.

Linear Measure

inches	millimeters
1/16	1.5875*
1/8	3.2
3/16	4.8
1/4	6.35*
5/16	7.9
3/8	9.5
7/16	11.1
1/2	12.7*
9/16	14.3
5/8	15.9
11/16	17.5
3/4	19.05*
13/16	20.6
7/8	22.2
15/16	23.8
1	25.4*

inches	centimeters
1	2.54*
2	5.1
3	7.6
4	10.2
5	12.7*
6	15.2
7	17.8
8	20.3
9	22.9
10	25.4*
11	27.9
12	30.5

feet	centimeters	meters
1	30.48*	.3048*
2	61	.61
3	91	.91
4	122	1.22
5	152	1.52
6	183	1.83
7	213	2.13
8	244	2.44
9	274	2.74
10	305	3.05
50	1524*	15.24*
100	3048*	30.48*

1 yard = .9144* meters
1 rod = 5.0292* meters
1 mile = 1.6 kilometers
1 nautical mile = 1.852* kilometers

Weights

ounces	grams
1	28.3
2	56.7
3	85
4	113
5	142
6	170
7	198
8	227
9	255
10	283
11	312
12	340
13	369
14	397
15	425
16	454

Formula (exact):
ounces × 28.349 523 125* = grams

pounds	kilograms
1	.45
2	.9
3	1.4
4	1.8
5	2.3
6	2.7
7	3.2
8	3.6
9	4.1
10	4.5

1 short ton (2000 lbs) = 907 kilograms (kg)
Formula (exact):
pounds × .453 592 37* = kilograms

Fluid Measure

(Milliliters [ml] and cubic centimeters [cc] are equivalent, but it is customary to use milliliters for liquids.)

1 cu in	=	16.39 ml
1 fl oz	=	29.6 ml
1 cup	=	237 ml
1 pint	=	473 ml
1 quart	=	946 ml
	=	.946 liters
1 gallon	=	3785 ml
	=	3.785 liters

Formula (exact):
fluid ounces × 29.573 529 562 5*
= milliliters

Volume

1 cu in	=	16.39 cubic centimeters (cc)
1 cu ft	=	28 316.7 cc
1 bushel	=	35 239.1 cc
1 peck	=	8 809.8 cc

Area

1 sq in	=	6.45 sq cm
1 sq ft	=	929 sq cm
	=	.093 sq meters
1 sq yd	=	.84 sq meters
1 acre	=	4 046.9 sq meters
	=	.404 7 hectares
1 sq mile	=	2 589 988 sq meters
	=	259 hectares
	=	2.589 9 sq kilometers

Miscellaneous

1 British thermal unit (Btu) (mean) = 1 055.9 joules
1 horsepower = 745.7 watts
= .75 kilowatts
caliber (diameter of a firearm's bore in hundredths of an inch) = .254 millimeters (mm)

1 atmosphere pressure = 101 325* pascals (newtons per sq meter)
1 pound per square inch (psi) = 6 895 pascals
1 pound per square foot = 47.9 pascals
1 knot = 1.85 kilometers per hour
1 mile per hour = 1.6093 kilometers per hour